What people are saying about …

7 FAMILY MINISTRY ESSENTIALS

"In this book, Michelle and Megan share lessons they have learned in their own leadership successes and failures. They offer practical advice to help ministry leaders shape growing ministries and develop amazing leaders. I can guarantee you will be challenged and stretched!"

Ryan Frank, CEO of KidzMatter

"Talk about *passion*! Michelle and Megan serve up some timely encouragement for church leaders, parents, and students alike to awaken to their God-given roles in the life of the family. *Immediately* translatable, these seven essentials will serve as a catalyst for long-range, transformational family ministries to be established, cultivated, and inspired."

Brent Eldridge, lead pastor of Arbor Road Church, Long Beach, California

"There has been no shortage of descriptions of why the church is failing the family, but rarely do we find prescriptions that help a pastoral staff do anything to change it. Michelle Anthony and Megan Marshman will not only make you aware of the challenges we face but also inspire you to equip and empower families for lifelong discipleship. I can't wait to have my staff and seminary students interact with their ideas."

Bill Staffieri, senior pastor of Beachpoint Church
and adjunct professor at Talbot Seminary

"With fresh vision and pristine clarity, Michelle Anthony and Megan Marshman guide children's and family ministry leaders through the swells of family outreach like a lighthouse on the sea. Mooring the modern family ministry movement to the authority of Scripture and a reliance on the Holy Spirit, *7 Family Ministry Essentials* is a challenge to every leader passionate about reaching the kids, students, and families to embrace God Himself and set sail for deeper water toward impacting the next generation."

Matt Guevara, executive director of International
Network of Children's Ministry, incm.org

"With a desire for health over hype, this book points us back to God's call to parents to lead the way in raising their kids to know Jesus. *7 Family Ministry Essentials* gives parents and church leaders practical steps for assisting each other in their high calling while ultimately trusting God for true transformation to happen in the lives of young people. I wish this book had been published twenty-one years ago when I started on this journey in youth ministry. If you have a heart for the next generation to know and love Jesus, read this. It is spot on."

Brian Holland, young adults pastor of
Purpose Church, Pomona, California

"In this excellent book, Michelle and Megan tell us why ministry to and with families is very different from simply adding more programs and activities to an already-crowded weekly schedule. They offer not only a compelling vision for family ministry but also plenty of examples and ideas for implementing it. I love their focus on spiritual formation and how we can create environments in the church where it is likely to take place. This book is a great read and will be an essential resource for anyone who cares about families and discipleship in the future."

Wayne Rice, cofounder of Youth Specialties
and author of *Generation to Generation*

"The days of entertaining youth ministries are over. Students today yearn for something more, something better than games, events, and typical youth group teaching. It's time to reconnect students to the church and help them hear from the Holy Spirit, and reinforce the importance of parents and challenge them to understand God's grand plan of redemption in relevant and real ways. No matter the size or style of your church's student ministry, *7 Family Ministry Essentials* will provide you with the guideposts that you need to reimagine and create a ministry that truly makes a difference. I'm so grateful for the contribution Michelle and Megan have made to the church and our ministry to young people."

Pete Sutton, director of student ministries at
Christ Community Church, St. Charles, Illinois

"*7 Family Ministry Essentials* is a conversation that this generation needs to hear in a culture inundated with consumerism Christianity.

Anthony and Marshman bring us into a refreshing dialogue, speaking about exploring abundant life through Jesus Christ *after* we exit the walls of a church building. This is not a how-to book, but a resource about families joining together to celebrate the salvation Jesus offers through the lives each of its members were purposed to live. The Lord invites children, students, all of us, to experience the ongoing narrative of His grand story in which we are privileged to participate—to strengthen, to grow, and to exercise our faith through committed family interaction. Anthony and Marshman's concern for this generation is evident and is what we need to be talking about!"

Chris Simning, international speaker
with Chris Simning Ministries

"Megan Marshman and Michelle Anthony are both women whose individual perspectives and opinions are difficult to ignore. In combination here, their insight into effective family ministry and its core dependence on God's Word and His Spirit is like the clear chime of a bell that wakes you up, calls you to action, and rings in your ears long after the last page is read."

Darin McWatters, pastor of teaching and
mission at First Baptist Church of Lakewood

"I spent years in ministry trying to be the surrogate family for my students. This book eloquently displays the biblical need of supporting and making the family the central foundation in a student's life. The practical guide and intriguing stories will bless not only your ministry but also the families that are a part of it. *7 Family Ministry Essentials* will help refocus the need of any youth ministry to not try to replace the family unit but to come alongside and engage it. Megan and Michelle lay an unshakable, biblical foundation of how to strengthen the families in your ministry. There is no way to have a stronger ministry than to have it supported by the entire family."

Evan Liewer, director of youth and young adults at Forest Home Christian Camp and Conference Centers

"There is a most incredible fresh breeze of the Spirit of God in the church with family ministry. Michelle Anthony and Megan Marshman are not only key leaders in this movement, but they also know and understand the powerful, generational transformation that takes place with family ministry through children's and student ministries. This book is a manifesto for the church on how to reach the hearts and minds of this generation. When you reach the family, you reach the world, and this book helps you do just that."

Jim Burns, PhD, president of HomeWord and author of *Pass It On*

"Megan and Michelle live and breathe a passion for the gospel and for ministry to families. This book is overflowing with that passion along with critical content and tools for accomplishing this goal. Their well-thought and creative communication combined with practical and biblical family ministry essentials are keys to reaching an upcoming generation with a lifelong faith. *7 Family Ministry Essentials* is a crucial read in a time in our culture where community within the local church and within our homes is vital for creating spiritually healthy families."

Scott Belon, high school pastor, EvFree Fullerton

7 FAMILY MINISTRY ESSENTIALS

A Strategy for Culture
Change in Children's
and Student Ministries

MICHELLE ANTHONY & MEGAN MARSHMAN

David C Cook®

transforming lives together

7 FAMILY MINISTRY ESSENTIALS
Published by David C Cook
4050 Lee Vance View
Colorado Springs, CO 80918 U.S.A.

David C Cook Distribution Canada
55 Woodslee Avenue, Paris, Ontario, Canada N3L 3E5

David C Cook U.K., Kingsway Communications
Eastbourne, East Sussex BN23 6NT, England

The graphic circle C logo is a registered trademark of David C Cook.

The website addresses recommended throughout this book are offered as a
resource to you. These websites are not intended in any way to be or imply an
endorsement on the part of David C Cook, nor do we vouch for their content.

LCCN 2014957981
ISBN 978-0-7814-1297-1
eISBN 978-1-4347-0933-2

The Team: Alex Field, Carly Lohrmann, Karen Lee-Thorp,
Amy Konyndyk, Jack Campbell, Karen Athen
Cover Design: Nick Lee

Printed in the United States of America
First Edition 2015

2 3 4 5 6 7 8 9 10

123015

CONTENTS

FOREWORD

Dr. Michelle Anthony has become a tour de force on her mission to equip this generation's families and church leaders with the resources required for genuine transformation through intentional discipleship. In *7 Family Ministry Essentials*, Dr. Anthony gently but deftly dismantles the juggernaut of today's well-intentioned but fatally flawed family ministry models by exposing their biblical insufficiency and deflating results. She then provides protein-rich principles and examples of family ministry that is church equipping, parent empowering, and designed to nurture authentic faith for both children's and student ministries.

Through her imminently accessible and intimately personal style, Michelle helps church leaders and parents reimagine faith formation in ways that resonate with clarity and authenticity. As an astute observer of her writing, I have realized that she is building an interlocking body of work through each successive book to produce a new and comprehensive paradigm for family ministry. Having been an eyewitness of her ministry impact in the local church and within her own family, I can attest to the fact that these principles are practiced by her and embodied in the lives of many. Let me invite you to drink deeply from the new wine that has refreshed me and many others.

Freddy Cardoza, PhD, executive director of Society of Professors in Christian Education (SPCE)

I chose to write this book with Megan Fate Marshman because she lives her life in such a way that embodies the gospel. Many leaders are talking, writing, and creating programs "about" the gospel, but few often see it and live it as being central to their ministry endeavors. Megan does.

Megan is a prolific speaker and has gained the reputation of authentic truth telling when she teaches. Her unconventional style and winsome words endear her audience to the soulful plea of her unwavering message: "Do you *know* Jesus? Have you received the good news in His gospel?" She is clear that when you do, everything will change.

Megan is a prominent voice for this generation, from adolescents to grandparents. With years of experience speaking to and leading thousands of students and their leaders, she is timelessly aware that the gospel has no age. No boundaries. No limits. To invest in Megan to write such a book is to reach into a generation of lives to whom I may never speak. Her influence is great, and while this book may be her first, you can be sure that it will not be her last.

Dr. Michelle Anthony, 2015

1

WHAT IF WE WERE INVITED INTO SOMETHING BIG?

A Look at the Family Ministry Movement

You are never too old to set a new goal or to dream a new dream.[1]
Les Brown

Every day, countless young people leave the church, and worse, they abandon their faith for something "more." Why does this happen, and what can we do as leaders to help young people stay on God's path? Create more programs? Use better curriculum? Provide stricter accountability to godly behavior? Perhaps, but first it is our responsibility to assess the ways we portray Christ's call to faith.

If we want to form spiritually minded children and students who own a vibrant, lifetime faith, we must begin by looking closely in the mirror.

Leaders must recognize that we may have been led to believe faith is simply *knowing the right information* about Christ and *acting with good behavior*—and we may unintentionally lead others to hold that same wrong belief.

Intellectually we understand that faith is more than knowledge and good morals. We certainly desire for those we lead to possess a robust faith that impacts every aspect of life, and we hunger to see faith that transcends childhood belief into lifelong faith.

In order to accomplish these things in a new generation, let's pick up that mirror and take a critical look for a moment. What do we *actually do* with our time, energy, and resources? Because if faith is simply about good teaching and proper behavior, then the church *is* a sufficient place for children and students to learn that. But if faith is that *plus more*—if it is understanding how to *live out* what we believe by the power of God's Spirit, then the family (with spiritually minded parents) is the best place for that!

FOSTERING FAITH THAT LASTS

If we are honest, what we say *we believe* and what *we do* often are not congruent. The physical building of the church and its abundant programs are often not adequate for fostering faith that lasts. And we were not the ones who came to this conclusion, either. Our youth did. They have been telling us with their absence and apathy for decades now.

Genuine faith is established when someone has a *firm conviction* (not just "good information") and chooses to *personally surrender* all rights and privileges of his or her life in submission to God (not just "behaves well"). Both the conviction and the surrender in our lives involve a supernatural transformation God does within us as we choose to obey Him one step at a time. And often along the way, we misstep, which is why grace is such an important part of faith.

NEW WINESKINS

In many ways, making an intentional paradigm shift from "achieving proper behavior" to "a lifetime of faith formation from a surrendered heart" in the ministries for our children and students could be compared to Jesus's words about embracing a new wineskin:

> Neither do people pour new wine into old wineskins. If they do, the skins will burst; the wine will run out and the wineskins will be ruined. No, they pour new wine into new wineskins, and both are preserved. (Matt. 9:17)

His original audience would have understood that a wineskin expanded during the fermentation process of new wine. This expansion occurred only when the bladder was fresh and pliable. Once expanded, it dried out. Putting new wine into an old wineskin caused the old skin to crack or burst open.

Jesus used this image to compare the prevalent religious system in His culture with the "new wine" He was about to pour out on the cross. The new wine was an opportunity for people to no longer have to "earn" a right relationship with God through observance of the law but rather to "experience" God in a relationship through the power of His Spirit, who was poured out after Christ's death satisfied sin's debt.

This paradigm shift in thinking (and acting) required a new understanding. The old ways of doing things were no longer useful for what was to come. In fact, those not interested in the new wineskin would lose out on drinking the new wine, which would usher in freedom and acceptance in a relationship with God.

BAG OF TRICKS

You may read that passage of Scripture and say, "Who would be foolish enough to pass up a new thing God is doing?" Well, in fact, I am. Perhaps you are too.

Perhaps you went into ministry with unbridled passion, or maybe you signed up reluctantly and then quickly found that nothing else would satisfy what you were created to do. Whether you were mentored or you stumbled upon your niche through trial and error, eventually all of us involved in ministry arrived at "what works." I call it our "ministry bag of tricks." The longer you have been in ministry, the bigger your bag! In our hearts, we want to see lives changed. We are passionate about it. We want to make sure we're using the things in our bag that *work*. We get nostalgic. We remember the ways God used the things in our bag—they were the things we prayed for, and He answered. We get very comfortable with our old wineskin. After all, it has seen a lot of miles with us.

Then one day God's Spirit begins to do a *new thing*; He wants to pour out a new wine. But we are skeptical. *Why should we change? It's always worked pretty well in the past, right?*

The moment we are seduced by the things of old, new wine is not ours to taste.

THE COST OF LAYING IT DOWN

There are practical matters too.

"How will my church respond to this new wineskin?"

"What if my supervisor or pastor doesn't agree with it?"

"What if I lose my job?"

Along with fear, insecurity can creep in.

For me (Michelle), I invested in the children and students in my church for many years. I was intent on faith formation as the goal. I was happy, content. But God was asking me to lay down my old wineskin *completely*.

God moved me to a new position at a different church. As I arrived, I was convinced that God wanted to pour out His new wine on this ministry, but I still warred against my raging insecurities.

As I took over the leadership of our children, youth, and families, I was tempted to show up on the first day with my big bag of tricks. Oh, was it ever big! There was hardly room in my office for me or anyone else when this trunk of treasures arrived.

History? I've got history—in fact, here's a binder with event notes from over a decade ago, *just in case*.

Experience? I've got experience—here are my degrees, books, and events that I have planned in the past.

Ideas? Plenty of those—let me just find them here in this bag, somewhere. And don't forget how many people have loved my ideas in the past. *Just saying.*

For some reason, my new staff didn't care about my bag. Even worse was that in my heart, I knew none of it would work if God was going to pour out that new wine. Thirsty for what was to come, I put the bag aside. At first I kept it close, for security, but over time, it was all but eliminated from view. With the old wineskin finally gone, we were ready for what God had in store.

Together we watched as the new wineskin took shape, and we waited in anticipation and humility for God to fill us with what we needed. And He did! After more than twenty years of ministry to youth and their families, everything I was doing was *new*.

What an adventure! We prayed, and God responded—children, students, leaders, and parents were *transformed*.

The staff knew we needed a standard of measurement—not necessarily a review at the end of a lesson, weekend, or even quarter, but rather growth markers over the lifetime of a child's faith. How might we perceive faith formation if our view extended further than next weekend?

In part, what we needed for this type of evaluation required the very thing we wanted to instill in our children in the first place: *faith*. We needed deep-rooted, robust faith that God was at work in our ministries in order to succeed.

A MOVEMENT, NOT MERELY A PROGRAM

God is at work not only in our churches and families but also on a global scale. And He is *inviting* us to join Him on this incredible mission. Ministry leaders and churches around the world have the opportunity to align themselves, first to God's plan and then to each other, in order to reach parents, youth, and children with new veracity and focus.

In every country I (Michelle) visit, I find more and more church leaders united in one language: *family*. From Beijing to Santo Domingo, Mumbai, Cape Town, or Toronto, the message is about equipping the family at every age and stage. Our methods sometimes vary, our settings are diverse, and our structures seem unique—but regardless of history, location, language, and tradition, God's plan is being initiated around the world.

But all too often we find ourselves "looking down" at the lower narratives of our ministries and families and asking, "Does family ministry really work? Is it making the difference we thought it would? Does it genuinely produce faith that passes to the next generation?" After all, many programs have come and gone in the local church, and not all have produced results for lifetime faith.

Why is a family ministry program any different?

Well, *maybe it was never about a family ministry program at all.*

Maybe this global movement is about something *more.* Maybe it's about a ministry to families.

Ministry.

To.

Families.

A ministry to families allows the gospel to intersect with the harsh realities of today's parents, students, and children. It meets them where they are. The transformational gospel is God's idea. He initiated it. He sustains it. He invites us to play a part.

And yet, our very real Enemy is also on the move. He lies to us, attacks us, accuses us, and looks for footholds in our relationships with our spouses and our children. You can bet that if God is at work, the Enemy is not far behind. He will steal, kill, and destroy.

The fruit of this destruction is dysfunction. And because of dysfunction in the families in our churches, we oftentimes find ourselves simply creating yet another program.

GOD'S BIG PLAN VERSUS THE ENEMY'S EVIL PLAN

Take this moment to read John 10:1–14:

> "Very truly I tell you Pharisees, anyone who does not enter the sheep pen by the gate, but climbs in by some other way, is a thief and a robber. The one who enters by the gate is the shepherd of the sheep. The gatekeeper opens the gate for him, and the sheep listen to his voice. He calls his own sheep by name and leads them out. When he has brought out all his own, he goes on ahead of them, and his sheep follow him because they know his voice. But they will never follow a stranger; in fact, they will run away from him because they do not recognize a stranger's voice." Jesus used this figure of speech, but the Pharisees did not understand what he was telling them.
>
> Therefore Jesus said again, "Very truly I tell you, I am the gate for the sheep. All who have come before me are thieves and robbers, but the sheep

have not listened to them. I am the gate; whoever enters through me will be saved. They will come in and go out, and find pasture. *The thief comes only to steal and kill and destroy; I have come that they may have life, and have it to the full.*

"I am the good shepherd. The good shepherd lays down his life for the sheep. The hired hand is not the shepherd and does not own the sheep. So when he sees the wolf coming, he abandons the sheep and runs away. Then the wolf attacks the flock and scatters it. The man runs away because he is a hired hand and cares nothing for the sheep.

"I am the good shepherd; I know my sheep and my sheep know me."

Jesus is the Good Shepherd, offering us green pastures and still waters, restoring our souls. The Enemy distorts the abundant life and distracts us, enticing us to pursue a false abundance that leads us away from the Shepherd. Think for a moment about how the Good Shepherd and the Enemy are at work in the "sheep" in your church's ministries. How are families, children, parents, and marriages at risk? Who are they following? Whose voice are they listening to?

Today let's declare that our confidence is in Jesus, not our programs.

Jesus said He would build His church and the gates of hell would not prevail against it (Matt. 16:18).

BUILD THE CHURCH

Imagine I gave you a bag of small, interlocking blocks and asked you to build a church. What if there were only three blocks in the bag, though? What kind of church could you build? Or imagine I gave you thirty blocks. What would your church look like then? Why?

Some churches have very limited resources; others have an abundance of funds. If you are involved in a smaller church with fewer resources, you may think it's easy for a big church to work alone, because they have everything they need, right? Or do they? If your church is larger, perhaps you see small churches and think that because they have fewer "pieces," they work better together with other churches to meet the needs of families in their communities. But in actuality, every church needs something that another church offers.

Whether we have all the resources that we perceive we need, or we eliminate ourselves from genuine ministry because we haven't been "resourced" as much as others, God's intention is for all of us to work together.

The beauty of it is that if ministry to families is our idea, we have to create it with our limited resources. If ministry to the family is God's idea, however, *He will provide*. What a beautiful picture of family—churches joining together, regardless of resources, to support the needs of our generation.

Imagine what we could accomplish in family ministry if we joined together on this mission—not just small ministries, but big ones too. We all have something to learn from one another.

Often we see our ministries as our individual churches. But for a moment, let's step back. Let's consider the bigger picture and allow our minds to engage in what God is doing around the globe. After all, family ministry is the means to the gospel, not the end!

A BIGGER PERSPECTIVE OF CHURCH

Many years ago, I (Michelle) spent three months in Kenya, Africa. My husband and I lived in the village of Kijabe, doing life alongside the people there, intending to train Christian leaders on how to do church ministry. We confidently arrived there with our degrees and experiences, ready to help Kenyan church leaders. Yet God had a different lesson to be learned, and it wasn't for the Kijabe people; it was for us.

I remember the first church service we attended there. People traveled on foot three hours to be there. I was astounded; it was so foreign to me. Where I lived in the United States, people would barely drive across town to attend church.

As the service started, the pastor shared from Scripture for approximately ten minutes. The congregation cheered at the reading of God's Word. Then, for over an hour and a half, the people began to testify about what God had been doing in their lives in the past week. Person after person stood and shared how God had been provider, present, or faithful in their lives.

The gospel wasn't simply something they accepted in order to earn salvation—it was the very essence of how they lived their daily lives. They saw the gospel at the intersections of their moment-by-moment living.

At the time, most residents of Kijabe were paid for their work every Monday, so by Sunday, their resources were slim. Yet each person brought whatever he or she had left for a "meal share" (what we might call a potluck). One person brought half of a potato. Another person had a couple of carrots, another an onion, and one person even brought the bone of a lamb with a bit of meat left.

What they individually had in scarcity, collectively there was abundance. I walked out of that first service, looked at my husband, and said, "I have nothing to teach them about church."

I could only learn from them. They made the main thing the main thing—they sacrificed for God and for each other, and when everyone worked together, the result was bountiful and full of joy.

Shouldn't this be the picture of the church? Not one of us has "enough" on our own, but together we can bring healing and restoration to the families in our churches.

GOD IS ON THE MOVE

God has initiated a movement of family ministry around the globe, but sometimes we don't see it as a movement because we have relegated it as a *department* or a *program*.

Do we really see God moving? Or are *we* the ones moving?

When God is on the move, we see things with a different set of eyes. When we're the ones moving, everything is just a blur.

Remember the Israelites in the wilderness? A pillar of fire or pillar of cloud guided them through the desert. The Israelites had to pack up and move each time the fire or cloud moved. That type of faith and submission says, "God is moving, and we need to follow" and requires discipline to recognize that God is at work and that He is moving. Our response must be to follow where He leads.

When God moves, He helps us see things differently.

Pause for a second.

Where do you see God moving right now?

Or are you the one moving and things just seem to be a blur?

When we release ourselves to His guidance, we see afresh what is around us. We see opportunities, people, marriages, kids, students, church, and the mission behind all of it. He *is* moving … He is always at work to redeem, and we simply come alongside what He is doing. But we need to have His eyes to see it.

IMPLICATIONS FOR MINISTRY

Family ministry is done in the context of the local church, which is done in the context of the global church. We all have the same mission; we simply contextualize the message for our specific age groups, departments, programs, churches, cities, neighborhoods, and denominations.

Family ministry shouldn't be disconnected from the mission of the church. It's about accomplishing *the* mission, the Great Commission. Our family ministries must match our ecclesiology. Ask yourself, "What is the role of the global church? The local church? How does our family ministry fit into that?"

If we believe in our ecclesiology that the mission of the church is to bring healing and redemption to brokenness and sin, then our ministries to families cannot be simply "programs."

I (Michelle) am conducting an informal survey in which I've recently been asking ministry leaders to tell me about their family ministries. Without exception, they've all immediately responded by talking about the programs they offer. As leaders, we are conditioned to define ourselves by our ministry programs. It's as if we have ministry simply through "program osmosis."

We're distracted by our ministry programs while the world around us becomes more distorted. Remember these words?

"The thief comes only to steal and kill and destroy; I have come that they may have life, and have it to the full" (John 10:10).

The Enemy is in the business of stealing, killing, and destroying families.

Furthermore, family ministry in all its complexity has found itself primarily the responsibility of the children's and youth departments at most churches around the United States. But family ministry needs to be a *church-wide* mission because today's families need the gospel.

THE BIG DISCONNECT

How is it that we can be so passionate about the gospel, ministry to family dysfunction and distortion, and redemption, but if someone observed our ministries they would see our greatest passion somehow disconnected from what we do? Why is there such disparity between what we are passionate about and what we do?

I believe there are several reasons. First, if we make ministry about us and it goes well, we get the glory. When things go poorly—parents are complaining—we're failures.

But when did ministry become about us anyway?

This disconnect is a focus issue. I wonder if, more than anything, we need to redefine our focus in ministry to families as simply responding to the needs and brokenness around us.

Another reason for this disconnect can be the leadership above us. Perhaps they don't share the same passion for families and their brokenness that we do. Maybe they don't see family ministry as a vehicle to bring the gospel to today's individuals.

I (Michelle) remember a situation in which I was serving as the family ministry director at a church. One day the children's pastor and I were helping two single moms and their children move in together after both were rescued from physically abusive relationships. We were getting them settled in, ministering to the physical and emotional needs of the children, when we got a phone call from my supervisor.

On the other end of the phone I heard the words, "Where are you? Why are you both out of the office?" I began to excitedly share how God was using us, but I was cut off. My supervisor simply stated that we needed to get back to "work." As the family and children's ministry leaders at our church, shouldn't that have been our work?

We can get caught up in making it about the idea of family ministry instead of the reason or the why behind this idea.

How often do we become the poster children for family ministry in our lives, in our jobs, and even on social media and yet lose focus on the very real needs of families in our churches and communities?

When was the last time you got to do ministry to or with families?

Eugene Cho made a similar argument about ministry in the church today in his book *Overrated: Are We More in Love with the Idea of Changing the World Than Actually Changing the World?* He framed the issue in terms of justice. Cho took a trip to Burma and thought he'd come back with the inspiration to write a book or a blog on injustice. Instead he felt convicted by the Holy Spirit to give up a year of pay and use that money to actually *do* ministry. Rather than simply writing about it, he knew that God was asking him to sacrifice in a less recognizable way—one that would require him to determine if he really cared about this issue as much as he said he did.

During that year, Cho realized that as the church, we love ideas … until *personal cost* is involved.

So do we really want to *do* ministry to families, or do we just like the *idea* of family ministry?

What personal cost must we wrestle with?

Do we really want to make this sacrifice?

CREATING AN ENVIRONMENT FOR MINISTRY TO FAMILIES

A ministry to families creates environments where each family member can experience the abundant life that comes from pursuing Jesus. In this book we will outline seven family ministry essentials. These essentials will help you recognize focus areas that will begin to create a strategy for reaching a new generation—one that will transcend childhood beliefs and cultivate lifetime faith; one that by God's grace will bring the gospel to every member in every family around the globe.

These seven essentials are:

1. Empowering Family as Primary
2. Spiritual Formation for Lifetime Faith
3. Scripture Is Our Authority
4. The Holy Spirit Teaches
5. God's Grand Redemptive Narrative

6. God Is Central

7. A Community of Ministry Support

These essentials are a means to create a culture change—one that impacts the way we live in community with one another. It's less about "things to do" and more about "ways to live and think." When a community begins to speak the same language, is intent on common values and goals, and is committed to these things outside one hour of church on a given week, authentic change starts to take place.

In the final chapter of this book, we will discuss how to practically lead a new generation through the seasons of change that will inevitably arise in the pursuit of ministry to the family. Creating a spiritually healthy family ministry within the context of the local church and the home life of the modern family will not happen overnight; it will take a commitment to a culture change over time with sustained vision and faith.

In addition, at the end of each chapter, we have included a "ministry assessment" tool that will guide you through a process of listening and responding. We encourage you to take time to go through these exercises (either alone or with team members) and use the practical resources offered.

A robust ministry to families will not be created by simply "getting through this book," but rather we believe it will be the fruit of your surrender as you join what God is doing in the church at this time in history. In essence, *7 Family Ministry Essentials* was designed to be a guidebook for you to discover *His work* much more than it was designed to help you create more work, for the sake of simply working more.

MINISTRY ASSESSMENT

Listen

What factors impact why you can feel so passionate about God's heart and intent for family ministry but so often find yourself "leading a bunch of programs" or "running a department"? What could happen if you began to evaluate programs by how well your church was ministering to the family?

So What?

List the next steps that will take you from where you are today to where you believe God is calling you to be in your ministry to families. List the conversations you need to have, the decisions you need to make, the programs you need to eliminate, and the types of postures, people, and programs that will help you meet your goals.

Now What?

Sticky-note exercise:

　　1. Use yellow sticky notes to write down the various programs your ministry offers (such as VBS, small groups, family fun night, leadership training, discipleship retreats, midweek, Sunday school, youth camps, etc.). Use a different note for each program.

　　2. Next, use a new color of sticky notes to write down the real needs or struggles of individuals and families in your ministry (such as depression, loneliness, divorce, drug or alcohol abuse, inappropriate

sexuality, apathy, anger, etc.). Use a different note for each need or struggle.

3. Using a large piece of paper or a whiteboard, put your church's yellow sticky notes on one side and your church's colored sticky notes on the other side. Next, draw a line from each yellow note to each of the needs that particular program meets or addresses.

4. Circle the sticky notes that remain. Why are there unmet needs in your current structure? How might those needs be met considering your limited financial or people resources? Can you partner with other churches or parachurch ministries to match their ministries to the needs of your church? Or why do you have a program that isn't meeting the specific needs of your church? How can you use these programs to help other churches in your area?

2

ESSENTIAL ONE: EMPOWERING FAMILY AS PRIMARY

Cultivating Spiritual Families

> *The church must assume the role as a training ground*
> *for parents to be the soul doctors for their children ... in*
> *order to bring spiritual healing. Parents must learn how*
> *to really be present with their children and to create space*
> *for contemplation and reflection in their homes.*[1]
>
> Holly Allen

It seems that everywhere I turn, someone is having an inspiring discussion about family ministry and the need for spiritual parents in the home. If you are like me, you may think, *This is great; I get it.… But what about the parents? They are the ones who don't get it.* How can the church begin to make progress in family ministry if parents aren't as passionate about this as the leadership is?

Or why does it seem that most parents wouldn't dream of missing a back-to-school night at their child's school, yet so few make attending a parent-vision meeting at their church a priority? We need parents who are awakened to how utterly imperative it is that they disciple their children, parents who hunger for more than merely getting through the day.

We have the privilege of reviving parents' awareness of their roles by showing them this envisioned future. It's time for us to pastor, shepherd, be winsome, and be inspiring!

SENSE OF RELEVANCY

Recently, I (Michelle) was online looking at the wide array of self-help books available to parents. There is something for everyone: books on attention deficit disorder, bedtime, discipline, defiance, curfew, complaining, bed-wetting, biting, finances, friends, fighting in the car—an entire book about managing automobile arguments!—manners, media, potty training … You name the issue, and there is a book for it. There are even books that promise parents they can fix everything that is wrong with their children in one week.

These are the issues that control the very lives of our parents; these issues are *relevant* to them. As church leaders, our responsibility is to help awaken parents to their God-given roles, helping them see that the spiritual vitality of their lives and the lives of their children are relevant. Until they understand that, they won't assume the role they are called to.

The church is poised like never before to inspire and shepherd parents to invest in their children during these critical years of child rearing—including the middle and high school years, when some parents begin to "coast," thinking that their work is finished or that they no longer have a voice.

There is too much riding on this need for parents to lead their children in spiritual matters. George Barna said, "Every dimension of a person's experience hinges on his or her moral and spiritual condition."[2]

Think about it: What you believe and where you aim your heart determine the direction and outcome of your entire life *through eternity*. Eternity is at stake for all of us, including the parents we shepherd and their children. What is more relevant than that?

Parents often think if they hide in the shadows long enough, we will let them off the hook. At first our thought is that they are being lazy or stubborn, or even apathetic, but I've come to realize that most parents do want to assume their spiritual role—they just don't know how. They feel scared and insecure, because they, more than anyone else, know their imperfections. This is why we must graciously remind them that spiritual parenting is not *perfect* parenting, but rather *imperfect* parenting from a *spiritual perspective*. This means parenting with eternity in mind.

KIDS AND CAR SEATS

After high school, parents hand their kids the keys, tell them something parent-like, such as, "Be safe," or, "Make wise choices," and then they watch them pull out of the driveway, drive down the street, and fade into the distance toward college. For some, this moment is terrifying. Their children have been supervised their entire lives, living under the protection of their parents. But now, suddenly, they're on their own.

Both in cars and in general, parents of newborns are in complete control. They secure their children in car seats, and the babies can't see the road ahead. Then comes the first big change: the toddlers' car seats are turned forward. They start to see things their parents do and imitate them—again, both on the road and in life.

Once children outgrow the forward-facing car seats, they move to booster seats. From their high vantage points in the backseat, they begin to get a feel for the ways of the road. Think about the idea that many kids will spend more time in the car with their parents in one month than they'll spend at church in a whole year. That means parents must be intentional about modeling positive behaviors. At this stage of life, parents still have their hands on the wheels, and their children still sit in the back.

Next comes middle school, when parents introduce children to life in the front seat. It's no wonder middle schoolers feel like they're running their own lives, since they sit with the same point of view as their parents do. Many parents make the mistake of handing off the keys of life to their students at this point. But the reality is, kids are not ready for that kind of responsibility yet.

Developmentally, middle schoolers are just beginning to understand themselves and are therefore focused inward, judging their reality based only on what's right in front of them. Conversations between parents and their middle schoolers are vital at this phase to help children connect with the world beyond what's directly in front of them and to teach them to apply lessons learned from the insights their parents offer. Communication is an invaluable tool in shaping a child's ability to make healthy choices.

And then it happens: permit season. Teenagers excitedly take the driver's seat with adult supervision. Parents still are the primary influencers in the lives of their children. They're in charge of who gets the keys each time. This is a season of training, and parents have the opportunity to empower their teenagers with confidence while helping them navigate errors with grace and hope. This is also the age when some teens begin to hide certain things from their parents, depending on how their parents have reacted to their mistakes "at the wheel" thus far.

While teenagers are learning to drive, the only way they can get away from home is in the car of someone much older and more mature—ideally someone their parents trust. This is a major adjustment, and at times it may seem that these other older teens or adults have greater influence over teenagers than their parents do; but a parent's voice is still paramount. It's also important for parents to be in relationship with those who are riding beside their children during these formative years.

Then comes the long-awaited sixteenth birthday, when many teenagers are ready to drive solo.

And later is the moment when they nick a pole as they park. How often do parents, in the midst of their children's weaknesses, immediately strap them back in rear-facing car seats? Students need to see the love of their parents, especially in the midst of harsh consequences. That guidance and love will speak volumes once they're older.

Parents have an ongoing role in the lives of children as they grow, and so family ministries have an ongoing role to equip parents to be spiritual parents at each stage of this process. Parents don't automatically know how to do it, so the church ministry is a resource equipping parents to do their job along the way.

EMPOWERED FAMILIES

The church needs family-empowered ministries to raise up not only a generation of faith followers but a generation of spiritually minded parents as well. Parents today need the church to inspire them, equip them, and support them in this incredible endeavor. I (Michelle) now judge my ministry to families on how well I am equipping parents for their role in spiritual parenting.

We need a community in which we all hold each other accountable to these things:

- Parents will become the *primary nurturers* of their children's faith. The faith community will play a *supportive role* in this endeavor. All involved parties will acknowledge the Holy Spirit as the One who works *when and as He chooses* in the life of a child or student.
- The role of the church is to equip and disciple parents with the *same intentionality* that we have equipped and trained our volunteers in the past.
- The church aims to become a *family of families* where every member plays a role in the spiritual

nurture of the children and students in the community, recognizing that not all young people have parents who are able or willing to do this.

Let's unpack each one of these premises as well as explore practical examples of how they might look in a church setting.

EQUIPPING PARENTS TO BECOME PRIMARY NURTURERS

Most parents and ministry leaders don't argue the point that God's Word calls for parents to take responsibility for their children's faith formation (Deut. 6; Ps. 78). Nor do most have issue with the mandate of the church in Ephesians 4:11–12 to be an equipping entity. Rather, the problematic issue comes into play when we begin to discuss *how* this actually works in our current culture and society.

I (Michelle) reached one such point of tension in my ministry when I found that I had placed the words "We believe that parents are called by God to be the primary nurturers of their children's faith" in our statement of faith. I remember looking at this one day on our church's website and thinking, *How can I honestly say I believe that when I have done little or nothing to display this belief?* Furthermore, I considered the ways I had unknowingly sabotaged that value by having the church play the *primary* role and the family play a *supportive* role.

I also recognized the brokenness of the family structure in today's society. I was overseeing the children's and student ministries at the time, and each had its own set of issues that made helping parents participate—let alone feel responsible for their children's faith—problematic. Many of our children's parents were overwhelmed with the daily duties of raising children, and many were not spiritually mature themselves.

For our teenagers, we never saw or met most of the parents, and when we did, we found that many had "checked out" on parenting because they felt as if they were failing altogether.

We needed a strategy that would allow us to intentionally create a new kind of ethos that would help guide parents even when they were underdeveloped or overwhelmed. Here are a few examples of how God began to change our focus toward the family.

Take Home or Pre-Teach

We provided "take-home papers" after a child or student's time in Sunday school or youth group. While nothing is inherently wrong with a follow-up resource, I began to see that this sent the wrong message to parents. Without saying it directly, I was communicating that we would be the primary teachers of God's Word, while asking them to support us by reinforcing the message at home.

It was then that I became passionate about inverting the process. We soon created a pre-teach resource where parents would be the first ones to read the upcoming week's Bible passage to their children and interact with them on it with some basic questions. This allowed us to get both the youth and their parents in God's Word—something that benefited the whole family.

Then, when their children or teens came to church, we supported what they were teaching in the home and followed up with teaching on that topic. Now, instead of parents asking, "What did you learn in *church* today?" we, the ministry leaders, were able to ask the children and students, "What did you learn at *home* this week?"

Some may inquire about those children whose parents can't or don't engage in the pre-teach method. For them it's no different than the way we have always done it. If we change nothing, all of our children and youth come to church thinking that we are the primary teachers, and if we make this adjustment, we will at least help some of our families take on their role as primary spiritual nurturers. We have nothing to lose and so much to gain.

Faith Classes

As in many churches, our children and student ministries offer classes on new faith, baptism, and serving. Working from the "church is primary" perspective, I faithfully taught these classes in the past. Parents would drop off their children or students on Sunday afternoons with sack lunches in tow, then come back two hours later.

Of course they were grateful, faithfully did the homework with their kids, and brought them back the following week. At the end of the course, we hosted a graduation ceremony, and parents joined us in celebrating their children's achievements.

However, in order for parents to become primary, we needed to revise this model. We still offered these classes for children and students, but they would attend with at least one parent (or grandparent, uncle, or neighborhood parent). When they arrived, my role became to facilitate, rather than teach, the class. We made copies of the handouts with the "answers" in them for the parents, and the children had blank copies. By giving parents the information ahead of time, we set them up for a "win."

As facilitators, we did some instruction, gave examples, and posed different questions, but the parents were the ones who looked up scriptures with their children and teens and prayed alongside them. There was even a time set aside when parents found a quiet place in the church to share with their child how they came to know Christ.

As parents and children returned to the room, there was not a dry eye among them. I can't imagine the conversations that opened up because we chose to support the parents as spiritual leaders in their children's lives.

At first, our middle school pastors did not believe students would want to come with a parent (and they were correct; many did not). But as the culture began to change and parents were more involved in their children's lives from the preschool and elementary years, it became normative for our middle schoolers and high schoolers to expect that their parents would participate. It just took time and faithfulness in the same direction with a conviction toward creating new muscle memory in our students and their families.

Child Dedications

While this next one may vary in your church depending on your denomination, the concept is replicable. In our church we offer child dedications for parents who wish to formally dedicate their children to the Lord at a young age.

In the old-wineskin model, the parents would bring their children onstage where our pastor and elders would pray prayers of blessing over them. Again, there is nothing wrong with this, and in fact it is how I (Michelle) dedicated my two children. But as we considered parents as primary in our context, we wondered if there was *more*.

We tried many different options to allow parents to assume a greater role. We had them choose a life verse and blessing for their children that they spoke over them publicly while the pastors confirmed it with a supportive prayer. We also tried a separate service on a Saturday morning where families came for two hours with relatives and friends for an extended and focused time of dedication.

In the latter example, each member of the families—sometimes three generations!—received space and time to speak blessings over the children. Our pastoral staff joined them to offer Scripture and prayers as well as a time of fellowship. Our parents have been impacted in tremendous ways as they prepared for and eventually looked back on this special day of anointing on their children.

Parent Shepherds

If you're in student ministry, you've likely asked or been asked, "What about students who come from non-Christian homes? Are their parents still primary, and what is the church's role in this case? Or, how about parents who desire to get involved but also want to respect their children's wishes for them not to be around during youth group?"

Meet Dana Dill, middle school pastor and family ministry thought leader.

I (Megan) will never forget the first conversation I had with Dana because of his answer to the question "What's your strategy for youth ministry?"

"Well, God's strategy is family ministry, and God's strategy is my strategy."

Assuming he had learned this from attending a family ministry conference or sat under the teaching of a family ministry–minded professor, I asked, "Where did you learn this?" It turns out Dana listened to *the* family ministry leader, God Himself, as he expressed, "Well, I read Deuteronomy 6:4–7."

Student ministry is not exempt from God's design for faith repli-cation. Faith formation is achieved through the context of the family, and the church plays a supportive role in this endeavor. During times of brokenness, the faith community steps up to help. Broken and faithless families are not original to the twenty-first century. The church still plays a supportive and equipping role in this endeavor and fills in the gap for families when sin, spiritual blindness, or dys-function keeps parents from being spiritual leaders (Eph. 4:12).

However, what we say "Amen!" to on paper doesn't always translate into our ministry practices. Although our good ideas get talked about, sometimes they don't find practical implementation. The problem is especially true when we try to figure out how to empower parents as primary within student ministry. If this is true for you, then starting what Dana Dill calls a Parent Shepherd ministry may help.

Community through Adoption

Parent Shepherds can expose your students to spiritual parents, extend your students' web of support and care, and build stronger relationships between youth ministry leaders and parents. Here's how: Parent Shepherds are married couples who "adopt" small groups within the student ministry with the intention of helping them grow as disciples of Jesus. Parent Shepherds support their small group by practicing these three actionable steps: prayer, hospitality, and parent outreach.

Our students and leaders need all the prayer they can get. Parent Shepherds are asked to pray together weekly for their adopted small group and its leaders. Every month or two, the Parent Shepherds are to be updated with the prayer requests and needs of the students and leaders within their adopted group.

In such an individualistic culture, a little hospitality goes a long way—especially for students and leaders who have never experienced a spiritual home. Parent Shepherds are responsible for welcoming their adopted small group over to their home at least once a semester.

The third charge given to Parent Shepherds is to make an effort to reach out to parents of students in their adopted small group. In this capacity, they hope to draw parents into greater fellowship within the church and to create community among the parents. Do you have parents who are seemingly uninterested in hearing from their students' youth pastor or leader? As surprising as this might be, parents are more intimidated by youth ministry leaders than the youth ministry leaders are intimidated by the parents. Let the Parent Shepherds help other students' parents, because they have something in common: they're parents too.

Parents are encouraged in church to make disciples, yet often they struggle to find a balance in prioritizing their own families. Having them reach out as shepherds to other parents is a strategic faith investment into their own children's community. As God has designed parents to be the primary pastors of their children, we don't have to challenge parents to chase down students to make them love Jesus.

In fact, God doesn't call us to change parents; He calls us to love them and trust Him with the responsibility of transformation. Our role as family ministry leaders is to strategically affirm, encourage, and equip parents as shepherds to love the leaders, students, and parents within our ministries well.

A Blessing

At the conclusion of our children's and student ministry services, we offer a blessing to each child as a benediction. The word *benediction* literally means "good speaking" and is most often translated "blessing." Numbers 6:22–26 records the Lord instructing Moses to bless the people with these words: "The LORD bless you and keep you; the LORD make his face to shine upon you and be gracious to you; the LORD lift up his countenance upon you and give you peace" (ESV).

A simple but very powerful way to empower parents as spiritual leaders is to inspire them to give a daily blessing to their children. This can be a prayer that they pray over their children, although the language is slightly different. In a traditional prayer we commonly address God directly, for example, "Dear God" or "Dear Jesus." A blessing, on the other hand, often declares truth to children about God or the life He has called them to, such as, "May you know that God's protection and love is always with you" or "Go in His peace."

We began to model this for our parents at family all-church events and gave them the opportunity to do it as a community to build their confidence. We also encouraged them to place their hands on their children's shoulders, heads, or arms and look their children directly in the eyes when they spoke the blessings.

It is a wonderful time for parents to affirm their love by saying, for example, "Jered, your father loves you very much." Whether at bedtime or right before everyone leaves the house for the day, offering a blessing can be a lifelong gift.

Instruct, Model, Practice, and Empower

One habit I like to assume in equipping parents is an *Instruct, Model, Practice,* and *Empower* approach.

Instructing includes any teaching, framing (or reframing), Scripture, and expectations. But often we think that in the abundance of information there will be change. Not so—and this is where *Modeling* comes in. We must next show parents what this looks like. We can ask someone to serve as an example, or we can just talk parents through it in practical terms. We have to translate the information into their realities.

Next, we need to let them get their hands dirty while the instruction is fresh in their minds. Parents get to *Practice* what they have just learned. I've found that this works well in one-on-one or small group settings to create some form of safety for the learners.

Lastly, we need to *Empower* our parents. This is a charge to go home and continue to practice. It is our faith and confidence in them to take baby steps and to manage their expectations.

I remember a single mom who wanted to begin to bless her preteen son at home but was sure that he would want no part in it. I encouraged her just to take it slowly and to do what came naturally. I advised her not to think of this as an all-or-nothing campaign.

She later told me the story of how one night she simply told him by name that she loved him before he went to bed. After a few days, she stood at the door and shared her love but also recited a blessing from God's Word that her son would be strong and courageous at school. Later, she did this standing next to his bed while touching his arm. She rejoiced when she told me that he did not recoil from her touch.

Finally, she did all of this with the lights on, looking her son in the eyes! This empowerment, coupled with baby steps, culminated one night while this son lay in bed yelling for his mother. When she yelled back to see what he wanted, he shouted, "You forgot to bless me tonight!"

I think this is a great example of how parents can gradually make long-lasting deposits into their children's and teens' spiritual lives. Children will remember these moments long after they are no longer in their parents' homes.

The Most Important Part

The statement we made at our church about parents being primary allowed us to intentionally think through how we could play a supportive part in that endeavor. But the final and most important piece is that it's the Holy Spirit who transforms lives when and as He chooses. We must never deviate from this by thinking that if we invert our paradigm we will arrive at transformation almost formulaically. No! It will always be as we align ourselves to the Spirit's work.

In a letter to the church in Philippi, Paul shared how this process happens in cooperation with the Spirit, since He is the one who gives us the power and the desire to obey (Phil. 2:13). Therefore, our role in family ministry becomes to equip parents to cooperate and participate with the Spirit's work, to come alongside that which God is already doing in the lives of His children. What a liberating way of looking at the role of pastoring and parenting!

SAME INTENTIONALITY

The next area of investigation for us was the realization of how much time I (Michelle) had spent in developing volunteers and leaders. Think about it: there are volunteer and leader recruitments, screening, training, appreciation, follow-up, caregiving, and even discipline or removal at times.

Volunteers and leaders are enormously valuable; they are the backbone of the church. We couldn't pull off a weekend or midweek service without them, so we intentionally seek to develop them at every turn. But at the same time, we discovered we hadn't demonstrated that same intentionality toward parents.

Where could we invite parents into strategic places in our ministry, taking into account their busy lives? Where were we training and developing them for their spiritual roles in the home, and where were we offering our affirmation, encouragement, and caregiving to them?

Spiritual Parenting Class

One of the first things I started was a class for parents called Spiritual Parenting. (The content of that course is now available in book and

DVD form.) This course allowed me to share scriptural values about parents' roles in the environment of our faith community.

In those weeks together, we were inspired, convicted, equipped, and supported to take the next step. Over time, this course gave an identity and common language to our parent community, unifying us in the same mission.

My friend Patti started a Spiritual Parenting class at her church and was surprised at what God did: "I offered this class because that's what a good family pastor does. And parents attended because that's what good Christian parents do too. But then each one of us left *changed*. We were blindsided by God's Spirit showing up, training our hearts about what it meant to nurture children and youth spiritually, and we all left with a sense of awe and peace, knowing we weren't in this alone."

Since then, Patti has hosted refresher gatherings once a month to keep the conversation going. This has allowed her to stay in her role of equipping and supporting the parents in her community.

Family Nights

One of the most challenging decisions I made during this time of transition was to not offer a midweek program. Again, there is nothing wrong with midweek programs, and many fulfill the exact values that we are discussing here. But in our church community, this extra night out was a distraction to our family focus. The culture we were dealing with was literally preventing our families from ever being around the dinner table or at home together on the same night. We felt that if they had a night they would reserve to go to church, then we wanted to sacrifice that for them to just be together as a family.

We challenged each family to set aside one night and declare it holy. By this I mean that nothing could touch it and that it would be separate at the sacrifice of all else. We asked each family to share a meal together (around a table, not a TV) and to engage in fun, but also spiritual conversations or activities. We knew that in order for them to take this huge step of becoming the primary midweek program in their homes, we would need to support them with training and resources.

The resources came first. We created a magazine-style booklet called *HomeFront* that included ideas for recipes, traditions, creative activities, worship, storytelling, time in God's Word, prayer, conversation starters, and more (today, this resource is available digitally for free or in print form at HomeFrontMag.com). Each issue focused on one of the ten environments outlined in my *Spiritual Parenting* book (they are also found at the end of this chapter). In a particular issue, families would be able to "create their own adventure" by choosing activities that focused on one of the environments. There was enough to do in each issue that a family could use it for an entire month.

Then came the training. We knew that if we held a Family Night Training very few people would likely show up. So we simply advertised a fun Family Night for all ages. When families arrived, we had stations set up all over the church representing the different elements of the *HomeFront* resource. They were able to choose their own adventure and go to any station they desired at any time.

It was so rewarding to watch families play games together, make candles, pray, and discuss God's Word. At the end of the evening we gathered for singing and worship and then let them in on our little secret. We gave each family a copy of the resource and said, "Look how easy doing a family night is. *You just did it!*" With that positive experience and an understanding of what it looked like, moms and dads, grandparents, and kids all went home to plan their next family night together. And thus the tradition began.

A FAMILY OF FAMILIES

We all know and probably agree with the old adage that it takes a village to raise a child. And when I look at many of the children and youth our churches lose, I can't help but wonder if we have lost our "village-ness." What I mean by this is how easy it is to lead individual lives outside of community. As I look through Scripture, it is clear that God never intended it to be that way.

The ever-changing landscape of the family further isolates us. In my (Michelle's) latest ministry we had children from two-parent, single-parent, blended, broken, gay-partner, grandparent, co-parent, and foster homes. And I'm sure I'm missing some as well. The point is that equipping us, the parents, to be the spiritual leaders in our homes has never been more challenging or diverse.

Today's family ministry needs a mission that says the entire faith community will feel the responsibility of raising a spiritually transformed generation of children and students, taking into account single parents, grandparents, or children who are simply without parents to play that spiritual role. The reality is that many children and students don't have spiritually supportive parents. It is our hope that by being part of the larger faith community, this young generation will still experience authentic, organic, and life-transforming spiritual guidance from loving adults in the church community.

A couple of ways we can facilitate this is by broadening our understanding of parenting and creating intergenerational activities. Any class, serving opportunity, mission trip, or family event or service can include the option to bring along a mentor, grandparent, co-parent, uncle or aunt, or even a friend's parent.

As we help our families think outside the box about what it means to be family, they will be less likely to exclude themselves because of thoughts that their situation is less than perfect. And let's face it; while here on earth every one of us has a family situation that is less than perfect! It's not so much about becoming a perfect family as it is about pursuing a perfect God together.

A NEW GENERATION EMPOWERED

I (Michelle) recently had the opportunity to take a six-hour drive with my eighteen-year-old son, just the two of us. While driving, I asked him if I could interview him about the way his father and I raised him in the context of our spiritual home life. I said, "What kinds of things formed your faith and have had a lasting impact on you?"

Family Nights

The first thing he said was "When I look back on our home life together, one of the things I wouldn't change is the time we set aside every week to do a family night." That wasn't what I thought he would say, but I'm a big proponent of family nights (as you have already read). We put a lot of emphasis on this, but I confess to you that as a parent, that was the single most difficult thing I fought for. There were scheduling conflicts, bad attitudes, interruptions from friends, homework, fatigue, lack of interest, and just plain old laziness.

Of course, when your kids are little, every night is family night. You're all around the dinner table, and they're eating their carrots and their applesauce, and it's hard to imagine that life will ever be different. But when your children get older, slowly but surely they begin missing a few nights at dinner, and unless you tenaciously and intentionally claim that territory, there will seldom be time together around the family dinner table.

The Red Plate

When my son was one year old and my daughter was three, we lived in a neighborhood with a lot of high schoolers. I love high school students and had built relationships with many of these teens. Often, I'd be cooking dinner for my family, and suddenly these neighborhood students would show up at my house. So I had to begin making larger pots of spaghetti and lots of pizzas because I knew they would be coming over if I was cooking. One evening I was tired, and I looked at this group of teenagers sitting at my house, and I said to them, "Don't you have homes to go to? Do your parents not feed you? You're always here."

I was just trying to be funny, but some of their responses were sad. "No, not really." "My family never has dinner together." "I never see my parents." "I don't remember other than Christmas or Thanksgiving sitting down and having dinner together."

My heart sank. I was saddened by their comments, but the conversation gave me a glimpse forward. We get stuck in the day-to-day. But in parenting (especially when our children are little), the days are long, yet ultimately the years are short with our kids. I realized that even though my one- and three-year-old were at the dinner table every night, that wouldn't always be the case. So we set aside the sacred day. Sometimes it was Monday night, sometimes it was Sunday, sometimes it was Friday, depending on sports schedules or whatever else was happening. But we declared one night a week to be family night.

My son remembered the kinds of conversations we had and the things we did at that dinner table. Every family night, I took out a red plate that had written on it "You are special today." This was a tradition in our family. We would think of somebody to affirm for something that had happened that week, and that person would get the red plate.

Endings and Beginnings

When my husband and I moved away from our home a few years ago, we were five hours away from our college-aged children (I had recently become an empty nester, reflective on the season that I had just completed). We moved on a Saturday, and Sunday night had traditionally held the place as our family night. That first Sunday night I sat in my new house, sulking. I thought, *It's family night, but we're* not doing it. *After twenty years of family nights, now it's over.* I was mourning.

So I got on Facebook and pulled up my son's page, and there was a picture of him I'll never forget! He and his friends were sitting around a dinner table, and the caption read "Family night." And everybody had a red plate! He later told me he did a word of affirmation for each of them. He said, "I just made spaghetti and salad and garlic bread, and we did family night. None of my friends ever had family night, and I wanted to pass on what we had to them and affirm them." So the tradition of family night lives on. I'm glad I didn't give up.

WHO, NOT WHAT

In his book *Family-Based Youth Ministry*, Mark DeVries wrote:

> Almost without exception, those young people who are growing in their faith as adults were teenagers who fit into one of two categories: either (1) they came from families where Christian growth was modeled in at least one of their parents, or (2) they had developed such significant connections with an extended family of adults within the church. How often they attended youth events (including Sunday school and discipleship groups) was not a good predictor of which teens would, and which would not, grow toward Christian adulthood.[3]

These words are probably something that we know intuitively. If we look back on our own transformation, there is probably a person we associate with our faith formation. Yet we busy ourselves with getting our kids to events and programs and making sure they know all the "right" stuff. We can never underestimate the power of allowing our kids to be in relationship with mentors and parents who are pursuing God with passion and commitment.

IN ONE GENERATION

Think about what could happen in just one generation. When we look at how the church has remained relatively unchanged for so many years, we may doubt this is true. But let's consider other culture changes that have taken some time to adopt.

Recycling. I never thought twice about throwing an aluminum can or plastic bottle into the trash when I was young, but today's generation is intent on recycling everything. In one generation this changed.

Sunscreen. When I was a teenager, my friends and I put baby oil on our skin so that we would darken quicker. Most of the time, however, we would burn and then peel off that layer in order to tan better throughout the summer. As appalling as it might sound, we didn't think of the ramifications and dangers. Today, young children can barely go to their mailboxes and back without their parents slathering them with the highest SPF on the market. In one generation this changed.

Seat belts. When I was a child, my family took long road trips in our wood-paneled station wagon. My sister and I would romp around in the back while playing with our toys and then lie down in our sleeping bags when it was time to nap. Most cars were not even equipped with seat belts until the '70s or early '80s. Today, children are in car seats practically until their first middle school dance, right?

Well, maybe not that long, but a parent today would not think of traveling in a car with a child unrestrained for any length of time. In one generation this changed.

Think about helping parents become spiritual leaders of their children. Think about how difficult it is in our current culture to educate, inspire, and remain faithful to the cause. Now think about what it would look like if Christian parents barely thought about spiritually leading their families through every age and stage of their child's development because it had become second nature.

Just think, *in one generation*, this could change.

And *you* could be a part of this transformation in your church's culture.

MINISTRY ASSESSMENT

We have looked at a variety of ways to make parents the primary leaders in their homes, how to come alongside them in a supportive way, and the importance of relying on God's Spirit to transform as He chooses. Take some time to consider the ways God is prompting you to respond right now.

Listen

How can you come alongside parents to inspire them to instill faith that will last beyond the years when their children are in their homes? Write down one thing you sense God is speaking to you right now. It might be to get a book. It might be to call a friend. It might be to set a date for some training. It might be to simply set aside some time to pray. But choose an action step that you can do today or this week that will help you come alongside your parents in practical ways for faith development.

So What?

Take some time to respond to God based on the things He has revealed to you. In what areas will you need humility, courage, or boldness? How will your response reveal where your faith is at today?

Now What?

Perhaps understanding how to create a culture or an environment will aid your family ministry. Below are ten environments where we can put God on display in practical ways.[4]

THE TEN ENVIRONMENTS

1. Storytelling

The Big God Story gives us an accurate and awe-inspiring perspective into how God has been moving throughout history. It is the story of redemption, salvation, and hope and tells how we have been grafted into it by grace. It further compels us to see how God is using every person's life and is creating a unique story that deserves to be told for His glory.

"God has a big story, and I can be a part of it!"

2. Identity

This environment highlights who we are in Christ. According to Ephesians 1, we have been chosen, adopted, redeemed, sealed, and given inheritances in Christ—all of which we did nothing to earn. This conviction allows children to stand firm against the destructive counter-identities the world offers.

"I belong to God, and He loves me!"

3. Faith Community

God designed us to live in community and to experience Him in ways that can happen only in proximity to one another. The faith community creates an environment to equip and disciple parents, to celebrate God's faithfulness, and to bring a richness of worship through tradition and rituals that offer children an identity. Our love for one another reflects the love we have received from God.

"God's family cares for one another and worships God together."

4. Service

This posture of the heart asks the question "What needs to be done?" It allows the Holy Spirit to cultivate in us a sensitivity to others and helps us focus on a cause bigger than our individual lives. Serving others helps us fulfill the mandate as Christ followers to view our lives as living sacrifices that we generously give away.

"What needs to be done?"

5. Out of the Comfort Zone

As children and students are challenged to step out of their comfort zones from an early age, they experience a dependence on the Holy Spirit to equip and strengthen them beyond their natural abilities and desires. We believe this environment will cultivate a generation of individuals who, instead of seeking comfort, seek radical lives of faith in Christ.

"God transforms me when I step out in faith."

6. Responsibility

This environment captures the ability to take ownership of our lives, gifts, and resources before God. A child must be challenged to assume responsibility for his or her brothers and sisters in Christ, as well as for those who are spiritually lost. We hope the Holy Spirit will use this environment to allow us to understand that God has entrusted His world to each of His children.

"God has entrusted me with the things and people He created around me."

7. Course Correction

This environment flows out of Hebrews 12:11–13 and is the direct opposite of punishment. Instead, biblical discipline for a child encompasses a season of pain, then a building up in love, followed by a vision of a corrected path—all with the purpose of healing at its core.

"When I get off track, God offers me a path of healing."

8. Love and Respect

Without love, our faith is futile. Children need an environment of love and respect in order to be free to both receive and give God's grace. This environment declares that children are respected because they embody the image of God. We must speak *to* our children, not *at* them, and we must commit to an environment where love and acceptance are never withheld because of a child's behavior.

"God fills me with His love so I can give it away."

9. Knowing

Nothing could be more important than knowing and being known by God. We live in a world that denies absolute truth, yet God's Word offers just that. As we create an environment that upholds and displays God's truth, we give children a foundation based on knowing God, His Word, and a relationship with Him through Christ. God is holy, mighty, and awesome, yet He has chosen to make Himself known to us!

"God knows me, and I can know Him."

10. Modeling

Biblical content requires a practical, living expression in order for it to be spiritually influential. This environment gives hands-on examples of what it means for children to put their faith into action. Modeling puts flesh on faith and reminds us that others are watching to see if we live what we believe.

"I see Christ in others, and they can see Him in me."

3

ESSENTIAL TWO: SPIRITUAL FORMATION FOR LIFETIME FAITH

Christ Formed in a New Generation

The ability to be honest about desolation brings us to the end of our self-reliance, which in turn opens up space for God to be at work.[1]

Ruth Haley Barton

What comes to mind when you think of spiritual formation? Solitude? Reflection? Devotion? If you're honest, maybe *boring*? I (Michelle) used to have the impression that spiritual formation was for the holiest of holy people. The really, really spiritual people participated in activities or events that allowed them to become even holier than they already were. Not that I thought it was a bad thing;

I had just somehow associated holiness and spiritual growth with something unappealing or unattainable.

CHRIST FORMED IN YOU

But it turns out I was wrong. I now know better. I believe all of our families need spiritual formation. Parents need it. Children and students need it. *I need it.* And now that I understand it better, I *want* it.

I want holiness not because it makes me somehow better than others but because it means I am getting closer to Christ. It means I am becoming more like Him. It means I am "set apart" to do the work He created me to do. It means I understand Him more and enjoy Him more. Worship Him more. Love Him more. Holiness is less of me and more of Him!

But holiness is not found in some formulaic package of ingredients. It's not necessarily defined by what we do or don't do. Rather, it depends on *what Christ is doing* in us. This was a big "Aha!" moment for me. To see spiritual formation as something I was doing puffed me up and made me feel superior. To see spiritual formation as something Christ was doing in me as I submitted to Him was a game changer.

Recall the apostle Paul's words in Galatians 4:19: "My dear children, for whom I am again in the pains of childbirth until *Christ is formed in you.*"

Paul was saying to the spiritually young Galatian church that he longed for the day when Christ would be formed in them. He longed for this as a mother longs for the birth of her child. He was aware of all that had been accomplished to allow this spiritual formation to happen, and now he longed for that realization in the lives of those he loved.

The time is here and now. And, like Paul, I find myself longing for the day when Christ is formed in the family members in our ministries.

Paul sent a similar message to the church in Corinth when he wrote, "Though our outer self is wasting away, our inner self is being renewed day by day" (2 Cor. 4:16 ESV).

Now, I (Michelle) have reached the age where I'm well aware that my outer self is wasting away. But in contrast, I have come to understand more deeply the importance of daily renewal in my *inner self*, and I want this focus for the youth and parents in this generation as well.

Also contrasted in Paul's letter to Corinth are the temporal things with those that are eternal—death with life and the seen versus the unseen. Things that are unseen, that are eternal, that are not of this world—these are the things the Holy Spirit is renewing in us because of the Father's great love and because of what Christ did on the cross.

So in simple terms, spiritual formation is the daily renewal of our inner selves to become more like Christ through the love of the Father and the power of the Spirit. As a ministry leader, I call this discipleship. And I want to make this my focus. But it is easy to get distracted, isn't it?

THE GOAL OF FAMILY MINISTRY

Perhaps you're already on board with the idea of family ministry. Maybe you've considered how to include parents in the process of discipling their children and teens. But before launching into how to craft this type of ministry and how to train volunteers and leaders to minister in this manner, we need to be clear on the goal. Family ministry *for the sake of what?*

Most of us probably went into children's or student ministry because we loved children or students, right? So to create a ministry around *parents* is foreign to many of us. It's definitely a lot more work, and it's far riskier. If we are going to create ministries that seek to capture the *entire family*, then we will need to have clear motivation for doing so. I suggest that this be your goal: *Christ formed in you.*

When we think about the families in our ministries or the children and students in their homes, do we have a growing desire to see Christ formed in them? Do we long for this the way Paul did for those he discipled? If not, our first step should be to beg God to put that yearning in our hearts, first for ourselves and then for those in our care.

THREE TEMPTATIONS

I believe, however, that as this desire grows in us as parents and ministry leaders, we are at risk of what family pastor and leader in spiritual formation Kit Rae calls falling into one of three great temptations.[2] After years of dreaming or hard work in our ministries, if we don't see the results we hoped and prayed for, we may become vulnerable to the temptation to make our ministries about *something else.*

Temptation 1: Communicate Information without Formation

First, we are tempted to make our ministries about information, facts, head knowledge, and things we can measure. If children, youth, and families learn information, we may be tempted to pat ourselves on the backs for training them in the faith. But maybe we shouldn't.

Children can memorize Bible verses. Youth can learn how to defend the Scriptures, and parents can know a lot of "stuff" about God and where to find certain passages in the Bible. These are all good things, but they're not enough.

Until those things penetrate down to the core and bring about life change, they're simply not enough. When we succumb to the temptation of information over formation, we lose out on transformation. And transformation is measured slowly over time. So we need to have eyes that look more broadly than just an hour on a Sunday morning or a midweek gathering. We need eternal eyes that see what God is doing over the long haul and hearts that do not settle for quick results.

Temptation 2: Make Ministry about Moral Training

We can make our ministries about good behavior or "how to look like a Christian in ten easy steps." This has been tempting for me as a parent, because good behavior looks so much like faith on the outside.

In his article "How to Raise a Pagan Kid in a Christian Home," Barrett Johnson said:

> The gospel is not about making bad people moral, but about making dead people alive. If we teach morality without the transforming power of the gospel and the necessity of a life fully surrendered to God's will, then we are raising moral pagans....

> Do you teach your kids "be good because the
> Bible tells you to" or do you teach your kids that
> they will never be good without Christ's offer of
> grace? There is a huge difference. One leads to
> moralism; the other leads to brokenness. One leads
> to self-righteousness; the other leads to a life that
> realizes that Christ is everything and that nothing
> else matters.[3]

Certainly when children are young, moral behavior is indeed what we teach them. We tell them things such as, "Say thank you." "Don't hit your brother." "Tell the truth."

We don't debate them; we simply state the rules. In moments when we teach these things, we almost don't even consider our children's hearts, because these rules are just things you do to live in this world in proximity to other people.

But as our children grow up, we as leaders and parents often don't grow with them. A father may still tell his fifteen-year-old son, "Don't do drugs." "Don't have sex with your girlfriend." "Say you're sorry." "Be nice to your sister."

When we as parents do this, we continue to use moral behavior tactics at the stage when moral development needs to be transcended by spiritual development. In spiritual development the heart is what matters most, not merely the actions. This is when we need to let the Holy Spirit come in and act in our children's lives. Yet if we don't make that transition, we fall into the temptation of making our ministries (and our homes) about just being a really *good person*. But really good people are not what Jesus asked for. He asked for people of faith. And faith is so much messier (and harder to measure) than moral behavior.

I think Phil Vischer, the creator of *VeggieTales*, said it best in an interview with *World* magazine:

> I looked back … and realized I had spent 10 years trying to convince kids to behave Christianly without actually teaching them Christianity. And that was a pretty serious conviction. You can say, "Hey kids, be more forgiving because the Bible says so," or "Hey kids, be more kind because the Bible says so!" But that isn't Christianity, it's morality.…
>
> We're drinking a cocktail that's a mix of the Protestant work ethic, the American dream, and the gospel. And we've intertwined them so completely that we can't tell them apart anymore. Our gospel has become a gospel of following your dreams and being good so God will make all your dreams come true. It's the Oprah god.[4]

Temptation 3: Despair

The third temptation is simply to give up. Sometimes we look at our churches, our families, or the leadership above us, and we feel unappreciated. We feel criticized. We feel discouraged. One of the Enemy's greatest tactics is to discourage ministry leaders and parents. As I travel the country, I can't tell you how many discouraged ministers and parents I meet. There's a strong temptation to despair and give up.

Kit Rae offered me this insight:

> Often we despair in the very process itself because
> we don't see transformation happening. We wonder
> where God has gone. We wonder why we don't see
> faith like we want to see it or how others see it in
> their ministries. We don't see God working and
> so we lose the "through line" and begin to make
> our ministries about *other* things, buildings, decor,
> volunteer training, or leadership development. In
> addition I think we even stop seeing transformation
> in our own lives and we despair. We fake it and con-
> tinue in a posture that is nothing but a fabrication
> … but what we truly long for is something *real*, for
> God to show up!

People are leaving ministry in unprecedented numbers. And many would probably leave parenting if they could. What's nearly as bad is when we "leave" but stay. Think of the times we've "left" ministry but still showed up to work every day. Think of the times we've "left" mothering or fathering but still showed up. Mentally, emotionally, and spiritually, we've left. That's a problem.

We are at a point where we need to make a decision about spiritual formation not only in our own lives but for the sake of family ministry. Because the reality is that we are going to be tempted by these three things. The first step is simply to acknowledge these temptations, to give them language, because we disarm them a bit when we're aware.

LIFE BY DEFINITION

The next step in resisting those temptations is to unpack that phrase in Galatians 4:19, *Christ formed in you*. We don't need a high and lofty explanation of spiritual formation that only the really smart or really spiritual can understand. We all need to understand *Christ formed in you*. We need to be able to wake up every day in our families and in our ministries and say *Christ formed in you*. Let's look at each of these concepts separately: *Christ, Formed, In You*.

Christ

Christ is central to the gospel, right? He is the gospel. He is the good news. Paul addressed this in Colossians 1:15–23.

> The Son is the image of the invisible God, the firstborn over all creation. For in him all things were created: things in heaven and on earth, visible and invisible, whether thrones or powers or rulers or authorities; all things have been created through him and for him. He is before all things, and in him all things hold together. And he is the head of the body, the church; he is the beginning and the firstborn from among the dead, so that in everything he might have the supremacy. For God was pleased to have all his fullness dwell in him, and through him to reconcile to himself all things, whether things on

earth or things in heaven, by making peace through his blood, shed on the cross.

Once you were alienated from God and were enemies in your minds because of your evil behavior. But now he has reconciled you by Christ's physical body through death to present you holy in his sight, without blemish and free from accusation—if you continue in your faith, established and firm, and do not move from the hope held out in the gospel. This is the gospel that you heard and that has been proclaimed to every creature under heaven, and of which I, Paul, have become a servant.

I'm overwhelmed by the power of these words—the power that rests in this proclamation that Christ is preeminent over all. Listen to the richness of the words Paul used: *all things, heaven and earth, the fullness of God.* He is *the one,* the *firstborn from the dead,* the *resurrected one.*

He is the *gospel* that is proclaimed. He's *central.* A. W. Tozer once said, "It is either all of Christ or none of Christ! I believe we need to preach again a whole Christ to the world—a Christ who does not need our apologies, a Christ who will not be divided, a Christ who will either be Lord of all or who will not be Lord at all!"[5]

And yet I still find myself allowing other things to become supreme over Christ in my ministry. When we think about spiritual formation, we can't have *Christ formed in you* without Christ being central.

One of my favorite books in the Bible is Hebrews. It is a compelling argument set out to defend the legitimacy of Christ and the new covenant. Written to Hebrew people who were probably new converts to the Christian faith, the author placed Christ as superior to all other institutions and people that the Jewish culture held dear:

- Chapter 1: Jesus is greater than the angels.
- Chapter 2: Jesus is greater than any man.
- Chapter 3: Jesus is greater than Moses.
- Chapter 4: Jesus is greater than the Sabbath.
- Chapter 5: Jesus is greater than the priesthood.
- Chapter 6: Jesus is greater than Abraham.
- Chapter 7: Jesus is greater than the high priest.
- Chapter 8: Jesus is greater than the tabernacle.
- Chapter 9: Jesus is greater than the law.
- Chapter 10: Jesus is greater than the sacrificial system.

After an airtight defense, the author began to tell the original Big God Story, recounting individuals throughout biblical history who by faith chose the *greater thing*. Lesser things such as Moses, the priesthood, the tabernacle, and the law were the pillars of the Old Testament community. In fact, these were the very things God gave them. Yet even good things, given to us by God, can take false primacy in our lives and ministries if we're not watchful.

When I look at the book of Hebrews, I wonder what this author would say about our ministries today. What things have we made more central to the gospel than Jesus? Is it our buildings, staff members, worship, programs, or curricula? How can we go back to the centrality of the gospel and the centrality of the story, making Jesus the center of all we do?

After all, any other message we offer will not transform a new generation into the likeness of Christ.

Formed

In order for formation to take place, we have established that Christ must have primacy. He is to be lifted up and acknowledged in all things. No program, Bible narrative, or activity can be worthy of our time and energy if it doesn't bring our focus to Him. Now let's look at the word *formed* and what it means to be formed.

Information and Transformation

As we saw earlier, one of the mistakes we can make about spiritual formation is to confuse it with information. We think if we can get young people to memorize the facts and figures, and hide the words of the Bible in their hearts, then when they're older and no longer in our homes and ministries, they'll have the truth of God. Now, helping a young generation hide the Word in their hearts is a beautiful passion that every one of us should have. But if children and students learn information *exclusively*, that alone will not be transformative.

For example, Sunday school is often based on a Christian education model that teaches spiritual matters much like one would teach science, math, or history. There is another model influenced by the spiritual awakening of the Renaissance. I (Michelle) have created a chart to show a comparison of the two models:

Christian Education	*Spiritual Formation*
• Intellectual	• Experiential
• Dogmatic and didactic	• Subjective and intuitive
• Memorization	• Meditation
• Exegetical study	• Sacred study
• Corporate	• Personal
• Recitation	• Reflection
• Rubric assessment	• Personal assessment
• Application	• Response
• Extrinsic motivation	• Intrinsic motivation

While Christian education and spiritual formation are not at odds with each other, they do have some distinctions. I believe that much of what we are passing on in our church ministries is commonly a model from the educational side of things.

When we include some of what spiritual formation has to offer, both in the church and in the home, I believe we give our children and students a full view of their lives in Christ: both knowledge and personal experiences.

Bible Study versus Sacred Study. Let me illustrate a difference between the two approaches of Bible study and sacred study: I once met a young man who had not grown up in the church. He looked at my Bible with dismay. He saw that it was well-worn (even torn) and that I had marked it with every pen color and highlighter imaginable.

To me, my Bible is a study tool. I want to learn from it and understand it. I have marked up one particular Bible since I was in high school. It has seen many miles with me. When I open it, I am familiar. I shuffle pages effortlessly, knowing exactly where I am going and why.

This young man's approach was different. While I was raised with an emphasis more on Christian education, my new friend had been exposed to more of a spiritual formation model. He picked up his Bible before me with reverence. Before even opening it, he bowed to pray silently. As he turned each page, I noticed that each was pristine without markings. He spoke softly when he read a favorite verse. He saw the reading of his Bible as a holy encounter.

Neither approach is wrong. Both are good, in fact. But I was challenged that day by this young man's approach because he gave me a glimpse into something I had never considered before: *the beauty of the intersection between Christian education and spiritual formation.*

Let's briefly unpack the other categories in the chart as well.

Intellectual versus Experiential. This describes the main focus. In the intellectual category, educators are concerned with what is known and learned. In the experiential category, educators look to what is perceived and felt.

Dogmatic versus Subjective. This describes how we look at certain aspects of our faith. In the dogmatic camp, an educator is placing value on everyone agreeing to certain things in order to ensure that truth remains pure. This is often how doctrine was written and why we find so many different denominations within the Christian church—these groups of people were dogmatic in their interpretation of Scripture. Conversely, the subjective camp doesn't water down the foundational truths of our faith; they leave room for questions and not knowing all the answers. They embrace the mystery of God and don't need to have answers to everything.

Memorization versus Meditation. This describes a certain focus on God's Word, and both methods are biblical. The Bible commands us to "hide God's Word in our hearts" but also equally gives importance to meditating on Scripture "both day and night." To memorize means we can recall the words, and to meditate means we are reviewing what those words mean in a way that produces different thoughts or actions.

Corporate versus Personal. This describes how spiritual growth best takes place. In the corporate camp, we would say that going to church and being in small groups are the best ways to grow, while those in the personal camp feel that personal prayer, reflection, and Bible study—where we are most honest before God—yields the most growth.

Recitation versus Reflection. This describes what we do once we have studied or memorized God's Word. We can either recite it back to someone to show that we have learned it, or we can reflect on what it is saying and compare that to our own lives.

Rubric Assessment versus Personal Assessment. This describes how we measure a person's spiritual growth. One assessment has a rubric or standard of where a person should be at a certain age or after a certain number of years as a Christian. The other is more adaptive to the individual; it sheds light on a person's willingness and ability to grow rather than on a specific point on a growth chart.

Application versus Response. This describes what is done after hearing God's Word. Some teachers place emphasis on how they instruct us to apply what is learned or how we change our actions accordingly. Others, however, believe we should simply respond to God through confession, thanksgiving, or worship and He will instruct us on what to do next.

Extrinsic Motivation versus Intrinsic Motivation. This describes how we are motivated to learn, change, or adopt new approaches to faith formation. In the extrinsic camp, we are rewarded or disciplined for either adhering or failing to adhere to new information, while in the intrinsic camp, educators hope to inspire us to grow or change based on our inner convictions or love relationships with God, regardless of compensation or judgment.

A comparison of the two philosophies of spiritual education can be stated in these terms:

Christian Education

External listening—gaining knowledge through books, teachers, and resources

Obedience—changing behavior

Trying harder—striving to work harder after disobedience occurs

Spiritual Formation

Internal listening—learning to discern God's voice

Desiring to obey—wanting to follow God's voice

Obeying in the power of the Holy Spirit—recognizing that it's more about learning to abide in Christ

Both/And

We can glean valuable insights from the rich history of each approach. Each has biblical support. Each has something that this world will demand from us. Each offers us a piece of our lives in Christ.

It's often in the quiet places where Christ is formed in us through genuine relationship. The "information" is part of the fertilizer that allows the "formation" to take root. But too often we make our ministries about either/or instead of both/and. Yet it's in the marriage of the information and the formation that we have transformation. We need to blend these two things into one union and remind ourselves that the soul learns differently than the mind. We have to capture both with intentionality.

The Tension between Abiding and Trying Harder

We want to create an environment in which children and students with their families will learn to hear God's voice and will know it as *His*. We also want an environment in which they will *desire* to obey God's voice when they hear it. We can't make them obey it, but we can create an environment that encourages them to desire to obey it. We won't ask them simply to emulate rote behavior because we want them to desire to obey out of a relationship. We will need to model what it means to be in relationship with God.

While hearing God's voice and desiring to obey it are important aspects of spiritual formation, probably none is more important than helping a new generation live this obedience in the power of God's Spirit.

We don't want them just trying to obey, mustering up the willpower to simply *try harder*. For whatever reason, many people hear this as a three-point sermon: "God is good. You are bad. Try harder!" But this is not the entire story. Of course God is good, and we know we all have sinned. But the remedy is not to try harder; the remedy is to be encouraged and trained to abide in Christ and the power of His Spirit for transformation.

It's a lifetime journey to learn to abide in Christ, isn't it? Just when I think I've understood abiding, I find myself working in my own strength, wisdom, and fleshly desires again. Or I abide in one circumstance, and then in another I fail. This is a lifelong faith muscle that God develops in each of us, teaching us to submit to Him, and our children and students are on this same journey with us.

As challenging as it sometimes feels to abide in Christ, unless each of us chooses to obey in the power of the Holy Spirit, we will fail in the Christian life. Over and over, college students and twenty-somethings tell me, "That Christianity thing didn't work for me." And when I unpack what they're saying, I think, *Of course it didn't work. How in the world could we ever live out the words in the Bible unless we were empowered?*

When Jesus was leaving with the promise of the Spirit, He told His disciples not to leave Jerusalem. I can almost hear Him saying, "Don't you *dare* leave Jerusalem, or you'll be in really big trouble. Don't you dare leave, because until the Spirit comes, you won't *be able* to do the things I've trained you to do."

In the same way, unless our children and families wait on Christ and learn to work with the Spirit, they won't truly be transformed. The Christianity thing won't work for them. It won't work for us, either.

A Hidden Heart

To understand the crucial part the Holy Spirit has in transforming us as we abide in Christ, it's important to look at the condition of our hearts. John Coe, director of spiritual formation at Biola University in La Mirada, California, once said, "We are in danger of creating a 'hidden heart' very early in life. But it is when we see the true condition of our hearts that we recognize our need to depend upon God's Spirit to transform us and not simply fake spirituality."[6] As we shepherd children's hearts, we have to be aware of the way sin has marred the heart of every person since the fall recorded in Genesis 3.

After the first man and woman sinned, their eyes were opened, and they realized they were naked. In response, they sewed fig leaves together to cover themselves. When they heard the Lord nearby, they *hid* from Him. When the Lord called to the man, he said he was afraid because he was naked and that was why he had hid. In other words, as soon as the man and woman sinned, they understood shame. Shame led to guilt, and guilt led to hiding.

It's essential that we understand this path. Many parents have called me and said they were shocked and appalled that their children were lying and trying to hide their sin. Yet we do the same thing. I'm a professional hider of sin. At our core, we're all professionals at this. Sin enters our human hearts, we feel shame and guilt, and we're deeply resistant to facing that squarely, so we hide.

From Hiding to Healing

Our ministries and homes need to be places where young people can come out of hiding. And if the parents in our ministries are not aware of their own tendencies toward hiding, they won't recognize it in their children.

In the garden, God called to Adam and Eve. He sought them out and invited them out of hiding. And even when they refused to fully come clean, He acted in love toward them. In the first sacrifice of a life, He sewed together animal skins for them, because where there is sin, there is death. And as the cross shows us, where there is sin and death, there is the offer of forgiveness. When sin comes out of hiding, it can be *healed*.

The book of Hebrews tells us:

> No discipline seems pleasant at the time, but pain-
> ful. Later on, however, it produces a harvest of
> righteousness and peace for those who have been
> trained by it.
>
> Therefore, strengthen your feeble arms and
> weak knees. "Make level paths for your feet," so that
> the lame may not be disabled, but rather healed.
> (Heb. 12:11–13)

Discipline, therefore, is for the sake of healing. When family members of any age come out of hiding, there will be healing. But until we recognize the depravity each one of us has inside—this bent toward hiding—we won't be able to nurture an environment that invites others out of hiding. We'll be constantly shocked by their sin, and that reaction will only deepen their shame and drive them further into hiding. They know there's something fundamentally wrong with them. We need to let them know we understand that and we can deal with it in Christ.

In You

So we have discussed Christ in His primacy; we have considered the elements that affect how a person's heart is formed in Christ. Now we have the phrase *in you*.

In you is the magnificent truth that God went from being far away and untouchable, where we couldn't even speak His name, to dwelling in the very hearts and lives of those who call Him Lord and Savior. He made us His temple.

He has graced us with His presence, and we cannot flee from it. Where can we go where we are away from His Spirit? If we go to the heights, if we go to the depths, He's there. If we are in sin or in confession, where can we go from His Spirit?

He is in us and for us. Christ is formed *in us* through the power of His Spirit. What does His Spirit do when He's in us?

He does what you and I cannot do.

No matter how great we are as ministry leaders, no matter how eloquent we are as teachers, no matter how fabulous we are as parents, the Holy Spirit forms in each person something we can never bring about: *conviction.* It's supernatural.

In Acts 2, Peter preached after being filled with the Spirit. Verse 37 says that when the people heard what he said, "they were cut to the heart."

Now, you can "cut somebody to the heart" with a sharp dagger, and this would be destructive and painful. I think that's how we often approach others because we want them to feel conviction. But a destructive dagger is not conviction at all; rather, it is guilt. We use guilt because it often gives us the immediate results we want.

When you guilt someone into doing something right, you can get an immediate result. But let's be clear: that's not the same as transformation.

However, a skilled surgeon with a knife in his or her hand, carving away the impurities around a heart, is "cutting to the heart" too.

But this type of cutting is for healing and good. This is what the Holy Spirit's conviction does. It heals. It transforms.

Too often in ministry we use the tactics of guilt and manipulation because they're available to us *without* the Spirit. In that sense, they seem easier. But if we rely on Him who is inside us, then He is the One who brings about conviction.

So if we want a generation that is transformed, then only the Holy Spirit in us and in them can do that work.

Only the Holy Spirit.

MINISTRY ASSESSMENT

Think about this incredibly important thought: God has placed you in a position of influence over a certain number of people for this time in history. I pray that as God forms His Son in you, His influence will spill over into the lives and ministries you touch.

Take time to listen and respond to how God might want to awaken you to more in your life personally or in your ministry to children, students, and their families.

Listen

What might it look like for you to put *Christ formed in you* in the primary place in your ministry? What choices will you need to make in order to do that? What will that require of you? What will it require from others? Spend some time writing an account of your thoughts and reflections.

So What?

Take some time to respond to God based on the things He has revealed to you.

1. Is this a time of confession or celebration?
2. Is this a time for quietness and solitude? Or is this a time for you to have a conversation with a member of your team or a family in your ministry for support or encouragement?

However God's Spirit is speaking to you right now, respond to Him with a heart of surrender.

Now What?

Using the Christian Education and Spiritual Formation chart on page 77, guide your ministry-leader team through an assessment of where your ministry (to children, students, or parents) is today.

After your assessment, consider if there is a particular next step you can begin implementing immediately that will allow for a both/and approach to ministry and bring about true transformation.

You may want to use the following questions to help you discern where God is leading you in each area of your ministry.

IMPLEMENTING A SPIRITUAL FORMATION APPROACH TO FAMILY MINISTRY

Church Staff and Volunteers

- In what ways will we need to structure our weekends to accommodate creating space for our children/students to experience God and His Word?
- How will we communicate these goals to our parents and children/students?
- How will this affect the overall annual calendar?

- Are there any events, practices, curricula, or structures that *violate* these principles? If so, what are they? How will we go about revising or eliminating them?
- Are there any events, practices, curricula, or structures that are *missing* that would support these principles?
- What are we *willing* to give up or sacrifice in order to make this a reality?
- What are we *unwilling* to give up or sacrifice? In what ways have we been blinded unintentionally by traditions, existing practices, or curricula that we need to abandon immediately? How can we ensure that we are not merely adding on spiritual formation and family ministry but that we are fundamentally adopting a new approach to thinking and being?

Parents

- How will parents need to be inspired by this philosophical direction?
- Who is responsible for this inspiration, and how will it be unveiled and executed?
- How will parents need to be equipped?
- What kinds of events, information, and opportunities will be available to ensure that every parent understands the philosophy and has the

opportunity to be empowered to implement it in his or her home?

- What resources will be needed to equip and support our parents? Financial? Time? Staff? Outside speakers/resources? Curriculum? Website?
- What specifically will be expected from our parents?
- How will we communicate with our parents on a regular basis and give them updates?
- How will parents offer feedback to us?

Children/Students

- How will we inspire and communicate a new path of spiritual formation to our children/students?
- In what ways will we adapt our language in order to make sure that all grades participate and understand the path before them?
- What are the desired outcomes of our children/student communities in this paradigm?
- In what way will we solicit feedback from them, if any?
- How will we discern the diverse but complementary roles of church and home in this model?
- Who will be responsible for articulating each role in the life of a child/student?

ESSENTIAL THREE: SCRIPTURE IS OUR AUTHORITY

The Absolute Gospel Truth

The gospel is this: we are more sinful and flawed in ourselves than we ever dared believe, yet at the very same time are more loved and accepted in Jesus Christ than we ever dared hope.[1]

Timothy Keller

I (Megan) saw how God's Living Word could move someone when I met a redheaded ninth grader nicknamed "Crank." I first met Crank (whose real name was Katie) and her friends when I joined their small group discussion at summer camp.

After I listened to their conversation about how "close they *felt* to God" at camp, I asked each of them how God had personally revealed Himself through His Word. This question seemed tricky to these high school girls who seemed to think true life changes were the result of good feelings evoked from a mountaintop experience. The girls sat quietly until the youngest, the redheaded freshman, spoke up.

As she began to speak, each older girl interrupted, shouting, *"Crrraaank!"* Katie giggled generously but obviously still wanted to say something. I was confused by the older girls' sound effects but kept my eyes focused on Katie. She continued, "Well, on Tuesday—"

The girls continued to make blaring "crank" sounds.

I finally interrupted. "Why do you keep making those sounds and calling her 'Crank'?"

One of the girls spoke up, "Well, Crank dedicated her life to Jesus on Tuesday, and she's been keeping all of us up after lights-out at night reading her Bible. All she has is an old flashlight that has to be cranked, so every half hour, we hear it again … crrraaank!" They all burst into giggles again.

The seemingly shy redhead spoke up through their laughter, "I am proud to say that I made the best decision of my life! I *surrendered* my life to Jesus. Surrendered. And I can't help but stay up reading His words in my new Bible because I just *have* to know more about who Jesus is."

She didn't know all the facts, but she knew she had surrendered to Jesus her rights and privileges to live her life how she saw fit. She was now a follower of Christ and was compelled to read about this *Word* who had become flesh, dwelled among us, and given everything for us.

Jesus was on the move, teaching Katie the beauty of a surrendered life. God became her authority. While her upperclassman friends boasted in wonderful experiences and good feelings throughout the week at camp, Katie boasted in her nickname and how it defined her identity:

> Crank (noun): *one who surrenders her life daily to Jesus—and so reads His Word to know more of who He is.*

THE THING ABOUT AUTHORITY

Most young people are "fine" with Christianity in much the same way they're fine with a poster on their wall.

Try to live as best you can for God—*fine.*

Deep conversations about the meaning of life—*sure.*

But as soon as we start talking to them about obedience or coming under the authority of anyone other than themselves (gracious and transforming though it may be), they wander. The God they thought they knew required nothing more of them than that they be nicer occasionally. A God who requires submission—*no thank you.*

People typically understand freedom as a "freedom *from*" anything that would keep them from whatever they want. As a result, some people have submitted only certain aspects of their lives to God—such as past sins.

Many students I've met admit to giving their sin to Jesus to be free *from* sin and its eternal consequences, but they're blissfully unaware of the less attractive but vital posture of obedience. They're happy to give up that dirty, guilt-wrenching sin but remain presiding judge over what they believe is right and wrong. So these students end up reading the Bible for information rather than transformation through submission.

Why do we have such difficulty with authority? Where do toddlers learn to say "Mine!" and "No!"? Maybe the problem isn't found in just *those students*; maybe the problem is with all of us. If I'm honest, I have a *very* difficult time with authority as well.

I have a hard time with passages like 1 Peter 2:21: "To this you were called, because Christ suffered for you, leaving you an example, that you should follow in his steps."

God's Word challenges my walls of comfort. I bet if you were honest, you would admit to having a hard time with authority too.

"STEPFORD" GOD?

Think about someone in your life who has authority over you. How does that feel on a good day? How about on a bad day? What words would you use to describe your feelings toward submission in general? Do you like when someone tells you what to do?

I'm thankful God's Word doesn't conceal the shortcomings of the supporting actors that adorn its pages. Maybe the children, students, and their families in our ministries are not so crazy after all. Maybe we all, since Adam and Eve, have something in common—*a problem with authority.*

Adam and Eve, as we do, fell into sin as they tried their hand at being their own spiritual authorities. They ignored the way the Creator of the heart actually created the heart of humanity to function—as the heart of a worshipful being.

Whatever we choose to live for eventually becomes our authority. And have you noticed? Our friends, spouses, and coworkers make crummy gods.

A couple of months into marriage, my (Megan's) husband couldn't get me to stop crying. We were in the parking lot of our church when I realized that Randy couldn't fix me. We were both crushed. He had crushed me with his imperfections, and I had crushed him with my God-sized expectations. Randy couldn't fix what had gone wrong in my soul.

The moments I'm not under the *ultimate* authority of God (who alone can fulfill me), I'm under the *ultimate* authority of some other small-*g* god that can't.

Notice that I said *ultimate* authority. It's appropriate to submit to parents, spouses, bosses, and elders, because God has established human authority (Rom. 13:1). We must acknowledge, therefore, as we hold any position of authority, it is for the sake of leading others to the *ultimate* authority.

This is why it is absolutely essential to realize that submitting to Scripture is not submission to a set of rules—submitting to Scripture means having a personal relationship of obedience with God. It means putting your faith and trust in His character, His plan, and His power to fulfill it, as revealed through His Word.

If we go through the Bible and dismiss aspects of it, we end up creating our own gods. Theologian and Christian apologist Timothy Keller calls this god a "Stepford" god, who is "a one-dimensional, cardboard-cutout God you have created, and I hope you'll be very happy together, but it won't be a personal relationship. It can't be."[2]

This young generation aches to know that faith and trust in God really matter. Therefore, the question for us becomes how can we, as family ministry leaders, lead families to come under the authority of Scripture? How do we compel them toward a life of faith and trust in Jesus as their *ultimate authority*?

In order to navigate the oppression of the world and the tactics of the Enemy, these children, students, and their families will need to be given opportunities to live by faith as they learn to *know and trust God's truth, discern His voice*, and *obey Him above all else*.

KNOWING AND TRUSTING GOD'S TRUTH

The current generation is eclectic—they cut and paste pieces of various worldviews and philosophies into their lives in a confusing mishmash of conflicting ideas. They think in spheres and branches instead of straight lines, and they often hold fast to the idea that there is no absolute truth. They are different from any other generation, and we all are aware of the alarming statistics of these young people walking away from their faith.

This tells me that they have missed the truth—people don't walk away *from the truth*; they walk away *in search of truth*. When you know the truth—really know it—it transforms you. When you *don't* have the truth, it's as the ultimate truth teller said: "People loved the darkness rather than the light because their works were evil" (John 3:19 ESV).

Romans 1:25 states that ungodliness and depravity are a result of exchanging "the truth about God for a lie" (ESV). We do this when we allow society to substitute absolute God truth with human alternatives or relativity.

Many teenagers today believe truth is always relative to the individual and the circumstance. And yet many of the same teenagers will also call themselves followers of Christ and say that the Bible is accurate in all of its teachings. Apparently the Bible is true only insofar as it agrees with their desires or feelings.

TRUTH IS GREATER THAN FEELINGS

I (Megan) was at a wedding recently when a young man approached me and said he still recalled a message I gave at his high school four years prior. He remembered the funny story I told, he remembered me shouting, "Your life is not about you!" and he remembered that I had landed on my forehead trying to do a backflip; but he couldn't remember much else. He asked if there was a recording he could listen to because he had begun to notice a pattern of selfishness in his life that he wanted to gain control over.

He was surprised (as was I) that my response to his praise was to ask, "What does it look like when it's just you, God, and His Word?" He stood silent, stiff, and awkward.

He had hoped for a quick jolt of inspiration from me, but I wanted to know about his relationship with the living God. After a conversation-shifting cough, he jumped to a new topic.

As he walked away, I knew he felt unsatisfied, and my heart sank. I didn't have a quick fix. In that second, I didn't have an inspirational suggestion or challenge; I had God and an honest question, but he was looking for a good feeling without the need to commit to truth.

We need to make sure we're teaching truth in a culture that denies it. Without truth, people are lost, stuck with a compass that won't point north. With the popularity of moral relativism, with the blaring invitations from social media to "get lost in yourself," and in contrast to a strong sense that something is missing, this young generation may be more in need of the authority of Scripture in their lives than most before them. These young people *need* to become students of the Word.

Our task, therefore, is not just to teach children and students about God's Word but also to encourage them to investigate it. We must show them that submitting to God's authority as presented in His Word is for their own benefit. And we can be confident in this approach because the Bible *is* reliable and trustworthy and worth submitting ourselves to.

Once young people begin to explore the Scriptures for themselves, we need to grant them opportunities to "flex their faith muscles" in ways that bring validity to the truth they've discovered. In providing opportunities to put the Word into practice, we're encouraging them to be not only *hearers* of God's Word but also *doers*.

One way this can be implemented is by setting aside time during youth group or a Sunday service for kids and students to *do* ministry as they share their faith in action in front of their peers. When students experience faith in action for themselves or see it lived out in the lives of their friends, its power is engrained in them forever.

FOLLOWING JESUS

Why would we personally submit to Scripture as our authority? Jesus did. He accepted the Scriptures as authoritative; He obeyed. Jesus did not learn obedience from being disobedient. "He learned obedience from the things which He suffered" (Heb. 5:8 NASB). Jesus's entire life was carried out according to the will of His Father (Matt. 21:4; John 12:49; 14:31; Heb. 10:7).

Submit because Jesus submitted!

But is that enough for the young generation we are ministering to? Is it enough for a generation that says, "Jesus is a great guy, a teacher, a prophet, a sage"? What makes Scripture more authoritative than anything else? If it's not our authority, then it becomes something that just sounds good and makes us feel good so we can be good.

TRUTH DOES NOT EQUAL MORALISTIC THERAPEUTIC DEISM

God's call for us is not just about feeling good and being good; it's about bringing truth to a generation of students who desperately need this truth. And letting students investigate the truth of Scripture works because the Bible tells the *truth about God*. When tested, it passes every time. It shows us He is worth submitting to as our personal authority, because God's Word really is true in the deepest sense of the word.

If we have committed ourselves to this practice, then how is it that young people still think that the Bible is not worth submitting to? Have they not read it for themselves? Do they know the truth they claim to believe?

To find out the answer to this question, I (Megan) spent three months, while working at a summer camp, starting every one-on-one conversation I had with students by asking them to articulate the gospel.

Whoever starts the conversation sets the tone. So I decided, for these three months, to establish the tone by asking them to articulate the core of their beliefs. These students typically came into the conversation with an idea of what we'd talk about, but after the initial hello, I jumped right in: "While I do care about the details of your life, first, please share with me the gospel. I love hearing the good news. Who is God, what is sin, and why did Jesus have to come and die? And what do His death and resurrection have to do with your day? This good news has the power to equip you for whatever you're facing." In those three months I asked over two hundred young people to give me their best stabs at the gospel.

I found that students had rarely been challenged to share the core of their beliefs and, consequently, often didn't know how. The only gospel that over half of them described was so watered down that they had become numb—even immune—to the life-giving love of Christ.

Probably without knowing it, they were following what is called a "Moralistic Therapeutic Deism" faith. Kenda Creasy Dean defined this as a "moral affirmation, a feel-better faith, and a hands-off God instead of the decisively involved, impossibly loving, radically sending God … who desired us enough to enter creation in Jesus Christ."[3] Moralistic Therapeutic Deism is simply death in a quieter form.

Whatever pithy thing it may do *for* us, it does nothing *to* us. It can't transform us into people who are no longer under the rule of sin and death—only obedient submission to the blood of Christ can do that.

Yet those three months of hour-long coffee chats reminded me of why I had gotten into student ministry in the first place. Once most of the students became aware of their inabilities to articulate the essence of their faith, they became impassioned evangelists who were deeply committed to being part of God's movement in their generation. Students are cool like that.

THE ABSOLUTE GOSPEL TRUTH

Does the gospel make you smile? Can you remember the first time you got to share the good news with a group?

I (Megan) had been a volunteer in a youth group for nine years. After a few encounters of privately leading a handful of students to surrender their lives to Christ, I vividly remember my first time sharing this *best news of all* in front of a group.

I'm not quite sure why my friend Rich Baker, the youth director, thought it was a good idea to let me share it in front of an audience of a thousand, but nonetheless, he did. I can even remember the pep talk prior: "Keep it all about Jesus, keep it clear, and keep it short. You get to share the best news of all!"

Forty-eight long minutes and far too many rabbit trails later, the story of Jesus's life, death, and resurrection was shared. As I walked back to my seat at the conclusion of my unintentionally long-winded sermon, I can still remember feeling uneasy. Did I articulate everything the students needed to know? Was the message more about Jesus or the Christian by-products? Was I clear? Did the students understand what it meant to surrender their lives in response to the message?

Rich sat beside me. I assume he noticed my posture of defeat. I remember his words: "Wasn't that the *best*?"

"Huh?" I raised my head and took notice of the surprising smile on his face.

"I'm already excited to hear you share it again next week," he continued.

This leader believed in me when I didn't know if I trusted myself. I don't say this lightly: *that opportunity changed my life.* That week the two of us had multiple follow-up conversations with each other, walking through the essentials and nonnegotiables. Then, the following week I delivered the absolute gospel truth—the center and base and measure of all truth.

I didn't share a formula to feel better about life; I shared the news that is good enough to knock you on your back and that comes at the vast price of giving up control of your life. That next Friday evening at that same place called "victory circle," I shared the gospel again, and I've been doing so ever since.

I am still amazed that God gives us ministry leaders the privilege of having a front-row seat to see His transforming power. We not only have the opportunity to share the powerful truth of the gospel, but we also get to present *how to share* the gospel and give those we serve the *opportunities to share it.*

Without a clear understanding of the gospel, all we have is good knowledge and a whole lot of outward conformity—a husk without the nourishing grain. It's like pretending we're married to someone we've never met. This kind of counterfeit faith sends young adults walking away in search of some other "truth" that seems to work.

The truth of the gospel revives spiritually dead people. It gives life, not a to-do list of unattainable attributes. Young people need to know this. *We* need to know this!

THE BIBLE IS HOW WE KNOW

"Jesus loves me, this I know, *for the Bible tells me so.*"

Remember this song? The Bible is how we know the gospel. The gospel and the love it reveals are not the soft love of a song. The gospel is revealed through the Bible's description of a messy, pierced love—the love of Jesus. The true love that could count every hungry moment, every mocking word, every mark of the whip that He would endure … and then came to earth anyway.

He didn't stop at death; He also experienced God's wrath against all humankind for all time. And the Bible tells us that the power that raised the incarnate perfect Love from the dead is alive in us, bringing us back and redeeming us to our Lord.

But being redeemed to our Lord also means taking Him as our *Lord.* His Word, His Spirit, His power call us to surrender. We are called to daily deny comfort and follow our Savior into the uncomfortable. I can't think of a comfortable way to carry a cross (Luke 9:23), can you?

This is what German theologian and martyr Dietrich Bonhoeffer meant when he wrote these words in *The Cost of Discipleship*: "When Christ calls a man, he bids him come and die."[4] Following Jesus is costly.

TRUTH IS WORTH DYING FOR

We need to deal with any misunderstanding of truth in our ministries. Jesus alone said, "I am … the truth.… No one comes to the Father except through me." (John 14:6) and further, "The truth [I offer] will set you free" (John 8:32). It's not something that you just agree with, like the right answer to a math problem. The truth is Someone to know, to live with, and to be changed by, and if we let it, this truth can change us.

I (Michelle) often think of Stephen, the first recorded martyr in the Bible. I'm always struck by this young man's understanding of truth, a truth that he had no question about dying for. This man had the truth instilled so deeply within that *living his faith* was merely an overflow of knowing and trusting in truth:

> Now Stephen, a man full of God's grace and power, performed great wonders and signs among the people. Opposition arose, however, from members of the Synagogue of the Freedmen (as it was called)—Jews of Cyrene and Alexandria as well as the provinces of Cilicia and Asia—who began to argue with Stephen. But they could not stand up against the wisdom the Spirit gave him as he spoke. (Acts 6:8–10)

Later, in Acts 7:59–60, we read that before he died, Stephen even prayed for God not to hold the sins of those who killed him against them. Ultimately, truth transforms the way we live. What does it mean to live for our faith? It means to be *transformed* by the undeniable truth of who Jesus is, what He has done, and what He continues to do through us.

DISCERNING HIS VOICE

Just as Paul said that Jesus was "obedient to the point of death, even death on a cross" (Phil. 2:8 ESV), and just as Stephen was obedient to the point of death, we are called to live in obedient faith.

Obedient faith comes from knowing God through His Word and hearing His voice. When we have a relationship with God and come to know Him more and more, we learn to desire obedience to Him. This obedience is then *empowered* through God's Spirit, not through our own furious efforts. We take little steps each day to enter deeper and deeper into a relationship with God and to align our will and actions with His. This is obedient faith.

As leaders, then, we need to put our faith into practice by considering the focus of our ministries. Deuteronomy 6 tells us it has always been God's plan to have one generation bear the message to the next, but in many ways we have failed to do this effectively. It's time for us to wake up to faith and reclaim the territory in our churches and in our homes for truth, to allow this generation to put their faith into action, and to create environments that encourage them to put flesh on faith.

To do that, we need to make space for families to hear from God and help them understand how absolutely essential it is for them to make space themselves to hear from God's Word each day. No one can learn to obey someone they've never met. It's only by making the space to hear from God that families can learn the desire to obey, so that they can obediently and daily respond to the moving of the Holy Spirit.

Take a moment and recall the last time you heard from God.

If you had to use three words to describe what you heard from Him, what words would you choose? Did you hear loving affirmation? A convicting, gut-wrenching revelation? A reminder that you're not alone? When you last heard from Him, what was He saying to you?

Some of the fundamental aspects of a healthy relationship include not just listening but also speaking and sharing life together. We can have a personal relationship with someone only if he or she communicates with us. Therefore, we can't have this incredible love relationship with God unless we accept the Bible's authority and learn to discern His voice.

Unless it's authoritative, it can't convince us of what we really need to believe—that we are fully known, fully loved, and fully forgiven. If we reject any portion of the Bible as authoritative in our lives, then how could we, when we feel worthless, accept the blessings of our truest identity "in Christ"? When we feel worthless and read something in the Bible that says we're not, we won't *fully* believe it.

MODELING DEPENDENCE

If the families we serve are not armed with the fact that Scripture is reliable and can be trusted, they'll fall victim to whoever has the savviest argument.

This is what Paul commissioned Timothy to be aware of. In choosing to surrender to God, we're choosing a dependent relationship.

Who is your Timothy? Are you confident that you're modeling dependence on God and His Word to be alive and active?

It's a two-thousand-year-old problem. People do not need to learn how to act more religious; they need a personal relationship with Jesus Christ. And we, as leaders, have the opportunity to model *dependence on this relationship.*

This is essential because if we merely model our abilities to defend Scripture, discern false prophets, and submit to authority all without a relationship, we model a modern-day Pharisee who probably does more damage than good.

We can let down our guards and model authenticity, admitting the ways we've listened to competing voices and showcasing a bended knee to Jesus in response. Otherwise, those we lead will erroneously interpret that submitting to God's Word is unnecessary. They'll think, *Well, my leaders* know *better. They always have it all together.*

Understanding dependence has drastically changed how both of us disciple people and lead small groups. Rather than feeding people with *the answers* derived from our own life experiences, we invite them to ask *how* the Lord might be leading them to respond by listening for His voice.

Giving opportunities for kids and students to discern God's voice *inside of* your ministry's time together as a large or small group will only further their desire and intentionality toward listening for it *outside of* the walls of your church. What could this practically look like in a ministry setting? One way is simply having them close their eyes at the end of a message and creating space for them to discern how the Holy Spirit might be leading them to respond. This time would allow them to hear *from* the living God they've just heard *about.* This may require a less jam-packed program and greater dependence on the Holy Spirit.

FULL OBEDIENCE

The primary reason we as Christ followers must personally submit to the authority of Scripture is because the One we follow did. Jesus accepted the Scriptures as authoritative; He obeyed. And Jesus is not just our perfect unattainable model—He obeyed as our *substitute*.

We can trust in God's Word because whatever He is asking us to do through His Word isn't anything He hasn't already done *for* us. In the words of Bill Dogterom, professor of pastoral ministries at Vanguard University:

> All of our sacrifices and submissions are predicated on His sacrifice. We are not called to a life of sacrifice *for the sake* of gaining God's mercy and love; instead, we're called to a life of submission *in response* (not repayment) to God's mercy and love.[5]

Why does Jesus ask us to surrender our lives? Because He has given us His.

Why does He ask for our bodies as living sacrifices? Because He laid His down.

It's time to put to death the thought that we have the right to live as we choose. And it's time to lead our ministries in such a way that a new generation and their families live out this conviction.

MINISTRY ASSESSMENT

Listen

Where in your life might God be leading you to surrender control and come under His ultimate authority? How can you model dependence on God and His Word to the children and students in your ministry? Where in your program is there space for children and students to investigate the Scriptures for themselves? Are you creating space for them to articulate their faith in front of their peers?

So What?

Giving opportunities for children or students to discern God's voice *inside of* your time together will further their desire and intentionality to listen for Him *outside of* the walls of your church. How can you partner with parents in encouraging children and students to surrender their lives to God's leading on a daily basis? How can you give them opportunities to discern God's voice in your time together?

Now What?

Spend intentional time empowering and equipping your leaders with the gospel. Set up one-on-one conversations with key students, leaders, and parents, and ask them to articulate the gospel.

During your time together, equip them with how they can share the gospel, by practicing the elements that are included in it (God's perfection and plan, our sin, His sacrifice, our new lives in Him) as well as recognizing how it impacts their lives today. The gospel is both a moment (justification) and a journey (sanctification).

Use this helpful outline to arrange your story or thoughts:

1. *God*: Who is He? What is His intent and purpose for your life?

2. *Sin*: Who are you? How have you intentionally or unintentionally thwarted God's plan or rebelled against His holiness?

3. *Jesus*: Who is He? What has He done on your behalf? How does this change your life? The lives of those around you?

4. *Live*: In response to the sacrifice of Jesus, how will you live from this day forward? Who will empower you to live in step with God's purpose for your life? How will your life be an act of worship? A living testament?

For more on the gospel and how it can be translated into a compelling daily pursuit, read chapter 6, "God's Grand Redemptive Narrative," in this book.

ESSENTIAL FOUR: THE HOLY SPIRIT TEACHES

Empowered by the Source

The truth is that the Spirit of the living God is guaranteed to ask you to go somewhere or do something you wouldn't normally want or choose to do.... The Holy Spirit of God will mold you into the person you were made to be.[1]

Francis Chan

In his book *Forgotten God*, Francis Chan said this about the modern church's experience with the Holy Spirit:

> I'm willing to bet there are millions of churchgoers across America who cannot confidently say they have experienced His presence or action in their

lives over the past year. And many of them do not believe they can.

The benchmark of success in church services has become more about attendance than the movement of the Holy Spirit. The "entertainment" model of church was largely adopted in the 1980s and '90s, and while it alleviated some of our boredom for a couple of hours a week, it filled our churches with self-focused consumers rather than self-sacrificing servants attuned to the Holy Spirit.…

The light of the American church is flickering and nearly extinguished, having largely sold out to the kingdoms and values of this world.…

We are not all we were made to be when everything in our lives and churches can be explained apart from the work and presence of the Spirit of God.…

Shouldn't there be a huge difference between the person who has the Spirit of God living inside of him or her and the person who does not?[2]

Think about that question for a minute. Shouldn't there be a *huge* difference between those of us who have God's Spirit and those who do not? The answer to us is obvious, but the reality is not as clear.

What is vital, however, is that we live in the truth of a transformed life, not because we *should*, but because we *can*—and we *need* to in order to pass on a true faith to the next generation. There is too much at stake to merely scratch our heads and say, "Yeah, that's weird, isn't it?"

The children and families in our ministries are looking to us to proclaim the truth of Scripture and the reality of God's power within us. So let's take a look back at our roots, when this journey with God's Spirit began, and what possible implications it could have for our ministry to children, youth, and their families.

THE GIFT ARRIVES

Acts 2 gives an account of the day of Pentecost. On this day, the Jewish community from all regions gathered in Jerusalem for the Festival of Harvest (or Pentecost). This festival was celebrated in the summer to mark the barley harvest and occurred fifty days after Passover. Because Jesus had spent forty days with His disciples after His resurrection and was in the grave for three days, this event occurred roughly one week after Jesus's ascension.

His instructions were clear: "Remain in Jerusalem until the Spirit comes." So the disciples waited.

Unaware that this would be the occasion when God would pour out His Spirit on His people, the disciples joined with people from various nations and languages to celebrate the Feast of Pentecost. And then the gift Jesus had promised arrived: God filled the entire place with His Holy Spirit, and His power was among them. This was the gift Jesus had said would be better for His disciples than if He stayed among them. While not all the events of that day seem clear to the modern reader, one thing is indisputable: *God's presence changed everything.*

Peter spoke with unprecedented boldness. He declared that Jesus was the Messiah, the sacrificed Lamb, and the risen Savior. More than three thousand souls were added to the church that day, and the afterglow of it lasted well beyond the festival.

The chapters that follow in the book of Acts show us the holy unity the early church experienced, giving as each had need and gathering together for fellowship and prayer.

THE SPIRIT OF GOD IN US

Because of what took place that day, the Holy Spirit now lives and dwells among His people for good. He no longer rests only for a period of time on those who are anointed for leadership—He is within all who repent of sin and receive Jesus as Savior.

Ephesians tells us that the Holy Spirit is the deposit, or down payment, of our future inheritance, the mark that we are truly His (1:13–14).

In his gospel, John gave language to the Spirit's role in our lives: Counselor, Comforter, Teacher, the One who testifies to all things true (14:12–27).

Paul beckoned his readers to walk in step with the Spirit, affirmed His role as their guide (Gal. 5:25), and urged them not to quench or hinder His work through rebellious sin (1 Thess. 5:19; Eph. 4:30).

In the Bible, the Holy Spirit is most often represented metaphorically by fire, because He enlightens and awakens the soul and purges, purifies, and refines us. The Spirit is "quenched" when any act is done or word is spoken that is contrary to His character. Someone once observed that fire may be quenched by heaping dirt or water on it, just as carnality and sin will grieve and quench the Spirit if we are not vigilant.

Finally, one of the more tender images of the Spirit is in Romans 8, where Paul shared that even when our groanings are too painful or deep for words, the Spirit intercedes for us on our behalf (v. 26).

It's not possible to even imagine a life of faith without the indwelling of the Spirit. Imagine those in the biblical accounts who by faith chose to follow God without the provisions the Spirit gives us. How great is this gift of His Spirit, making us the very temple of His presence. It's astounding, isn't it?

THE HOLY SPIRIT AND CHILDREN

Despite all of this incredible knowledge about God's Spirit and His work to transform us from the inside out, I find that many children's ministries are skeptical about promoting His power and His position. Regardless of denominational differences, we can be confident to teach children from an early age that God's power is available to them, and because of it, we can all live the lives to which He calls us.

We can train them to hear His voice, listen to His promptings and tender convictions, and obey His leading by the strength and counseling He provides. All of these are biblical principles, but much of this first needs to be learned by us as well, wouldn't you agree?

I am constantly "a work in progress" learning what it means to walk in step with the Spirit and allow Him to lead me.

CHOSEN TEACHER

The Bible says the Holy Spirit is God's chosen teacher; it is He who causes spiritual growth and formation *when* and *as* He chooses. How does this affect our role as ministers? While there is nothing wrong with having Sunday school teachers or teaching pastors, it's possible that even that simple title could steal some of what is intended for God alone.

Several years ago at my church, we changed the titles of our teachers to be "storytellers" or "small group leaders" in order to reserve the title of "Teacher" for God's Spirit in our ministry. It may seem as though we were splitting hairs, and I recognize that it is the Spirit of God who gives the spiritual gift of teaching to some believers; but I have realized the power of language in the spiritual development of children and teens, and this was one place where we wanted to be very clear.

So if God's Spirit teaches, what is *our* role? We can think of our role as creating conducive environments that allow the Holy Spirit to do what He does best: *transform lives.*

Transformation is a supernatural endeavor only God can do; but we can partner with Him and come alongside what He is up to when we "set the stage." We can create spiritual space, or an environment, in which God's Spirit can move freely without distraction.

In my book *Spiritual Parenting*, I (Michelle) discuss at length ten environments and how we can create them as places to put God on display in young people's lives, giving them a chance to flex those faith muscles in the process. (I've included a list of these environments along with their definitions at the end of chapter 2).

LIVE IN, NOT MORE OF

There's nothing magical about these ten environments, but they help give language to and breed a defined culture in a church that desires to allow God's Spirit to move and teach. These environments are not things we are encouraging a new generation to be *more of.* For example, we are not asking students to be more loving, more respectful, or better servants. Rather, we want to create environments where students see love and respect modeled or where they have opportunities to serve and be served.

They get to *live in* a context where these things are evident, where they see God's Spirit at work in and through them, teaching and training them what it means to follow Christ in God's power and strength. Our youth benefit from the opportunities provided or from the "spillover" of the adults who are living in the Spirit.

Do you see the difference between the two? One approach burdens a new generation with *being more* and *doing more* in order to somehow attain a religious piety, while the other approach simply *offers more* of Jesus. It allows our children and youth to see more of God on display—to know more of His character, His goodness, and His love.

One way to look at this concept is to think of an environment as a climate. We often think of our family of origin in this way. What was the climate of your home while you were growing up? Was it hostile, punitive, and self-protective; or was it loving, gentle, and grace filled? Either of those, or any combination, shaped who you are today. That environment in your home led you to see the world around you through a specific lens either for good or for bad. The same can be true in our ministries—the climates or environments we set will or will not allow the children in them to be shaped by the things that are true of God and His kingdom.

While teaching and transformation are *God's part,* intentionally creating these environments becomes *our part* in ministry.

While we seek what God is doing specifically in the lives of each student and family in our ministries, environments serve as general places where we have seen God's Spirit move throughout history.

THE TEMPTATION: MORAL FORMATION

Why are these things important in the teaching process? Without the accuracy of truth that God's Spirit offers, it is easy to get off track. Without God's teaching, our ears can often hear that God just wants us to be good. To obey. No questions asked.

John Coe said the Christian life is about a certain kind of obedience and effort. It's the opening up of the heart to a relationship. It's participation in the vine. Dependence on the indwelling Spirit. Abiding in Christ. *This is our obedience.* This is what the spiritual disciplines are actually all about.

Coe said:

> I don't want to be a good boy anymore. I don't want to fix myself. I can't fix myself. I want to learn to give up on the project and open more deeply to Christ's work and the work of the Spirit in my deep. But I am still daily tempted by moral formation.[3]

The apostle Paul knew this would tempt us. He wrote:

> O foolish Galatians! Who has bewitched you? It was before your eyes that Jesus Christ was publicly

portrayed as crucified. Let me ask you only this: Did you receive the Spirit by works of the law or by hearing with faith? Are you so foolish? Having begun by the Spirit, are you now being perfected by the flesh? (Gal. 3:1–3 ESV)

Think of how ironic this is. *Who on earth would be tempted to be moral?*

We commonly think we are tempted to be *immoral*, but Paul understood that the life of the Christian would include both temptations. We in fact find ourselves in the temptation of moral formation. We have this little guilt meter inside us, put there unintentionally by our loving parents, the church, or our sinful human nature. It beckons us to want to make ourselves better.

We have the opportunity to allow a new generation to think differently—to think, *Yes, I'm sinful; yes, I'm broken, but* I can't *fix myself. Only the Holy Spirit can.* This will require our children and youth to have an intimate relationship with Him, to know Him, to hear His voice, to depend on Him, and not to get up tomorrow to simply *try harder.*

We need to be diligent, because the temptation is so implicit in our curricula and in the way that we speak. We often give take-home assignments for application that essentially say, "Go home this week and just … *be better*. Try to be kinder to your brother, serve more around the house, and be more patient." All these things are good, but they're just *not enough*. My fear is that, unless we take great pains to carefully adjust our teaching ministries, we may ultimately send the wrong message to a new generation. And this message will be abandoned because it simply doesn't work.

JAKE'S STORY

Jake has abandoned church—worse, he has abandoned his faith in Christ.

Once a leader in children's ministry and on the worship team in his youth group, he has now decided to "experience" God through nature, world religions, and a myriad of drugs.

"It didn't work for me," he says. "It's all good, but it just doesn't work that way. You don't just say yes to Jesus and then *poof* you're all sanctified and holy. That's what people said would happen, but it didn't. My life was and is so full of what you call 'sin,' and I tried walking with God. So where was He? Why didn't He clean up my sin?"

If we are not bothered by these words, I'm not sure what words would do so. These are the worst possible words we could hear from a "product" of our ministries to children and youth!

It is time for the church to take serious responsibility for the way we communicate the gospel, a relationship with God through Christ, and a life of dependence on God's Spirit.

Many of us can understand why Jake's perspective is skewed. While there are many things we want to correct in Jake's perspective, if we were to look objectively at the content and methods in our teaching ministries, do they not often lead to this way of thinking? As today's youth are connecting the dots of what we are teaching, are those dots leading them to join in on what God is up to or leading them to a life of trying harder in their own power?

Because one option is freedom, while the other is failure.

THE WIND AND SAIL

Several years ago, my husband and I (Michelle) had the privilege of owning a sailboat. For my husband, it was the fulfillment of a lifelong dream after decades of sailing. For me, it was my first experience on the sea in a sailboat. I remember the first time he took me out.

In anticipation, I prepared myself for an epic day on the ocean, the adventure of racing out to the horizon. However, when our boat left the safety of the harbor and hit the open waters … *nothing happened*. We simply sat there, bobbing up and down without even a balmy breeze. I shouted to my husband to make the boat go faster, but he just laughed and said, "There's no wind today."

Not long after that day, we went out again. This time I was skeptical about the adventure part and focused on preparing delicacies in the boat's cabin. Yet this day was different. As our boat sailed past the safety of the harbor, we slammed into wind and waves stronger than I had never seen. My husband scrambled to get our sails into position, and off we went like a speedboat into the open waters. The boat was heeling while chips and salsa flew through the air. I shouted to my husband to make the boat slow down, but he just laughed and said, "I can't—the wind is in charge today."

As ministers of Christ, I believe our job is simply to hoist our sails as far and as wide as we can and catch the wind of God. That sail is important, but not nearly as important as the wind. When we allow God's Spirit to be captain and we submit to Him to chart the course ahead, we get a sense of what it means to depend on Him and wait for His Spirit to *blow*.

Of course we can choose to take down our sails at any point and motor in our own direction at our own pace, but that is not the life of Christianity. That is not the life that will be compelling for this generation, either. Once you're awakened to the wind, nothing else will satisfy.

MINISTRY SAILS

What are the "sails" in our current ministries? These things allow the Spirit to move powerfully in our midst, but we need to keep in mind that they are merely there for His use, *when and as He chooses.*

Some ministry sails may include programs, positions, room decor or resources, ministry themes, curricula, and other structures. When we look at the role the Spirit may want to assume in our ministries, how can we begin to assess each of these in light of His presence?

One such assessment led us to remove our children's ministry Bible Buck Store and our youth ministry video game wall in order to create a prayer and worship center for parents and their children to visit before and after church service.

As you can imagine, I wasn't very popular the day we took out all the cool toys and replaced them with a dimly lit worship station. Now I'm not against being or having fun or engaging in relevant activities for today's youth, but I wanted to proclaim that this time to be with God was sacred or different from what the world had to offer. And over time the youth and parents began to crave it and be changed by it!

As you walked into our children's and youth ministry areas, now you could see places where families could worship together. Family members could write prayers and post them on a prayer wall, give financial offerings, or write a declaration of God's character on a stone of remembrance.

FAMILIES LEARNING TOGETHER

One day, right before the church service began, a young single mom came in with her son and told me (Michelle) it was her first time there. She said, "In fact, it's my first time to church since I was a little girl." She went on to say, "I'm not good at this; I don't know what to do." Instead of inviting her to step right up to my Bible Buck Store or invite her little boy to play a video game, I was now able to lead her to the cross and prayer wall. I said, "You can pray with your son here, and I'll show you how."

I asked if there was something that I could pray about for them, and right there we paused to pray. I watched as she held her son's hand in hers, praying with him. I wondered if this was the first time this little family had ever done this.

She went to church, and her son stayed in our ministry. Later, during our time of worship, we invited the students to go to any of the worship response stations around the room. I watched as that little boy got up, went straight to the cross he had been at with his mom, and began to pray. When his mom came to pick him up after service, he took her to the cross and said with excitement, "Mom, during church I prayed again here just like we did before, and I know God hears our prayers."

As she left, she said to me, "You know, I've heard about Jesus my entire life, but today was the first day that I *experienced* Him. Thank you."

That was all I needed to propel me to look at other things in my ministry through the lens of "What environment am I really creating for the Holy Spirit to teach?" In this example, a Bible Buck Store wasn't bad, but it didn't facilitate the environment I wanted to create where children and their parents could experience God's Spirit.

DREAMING OF MORE

Once my ministry staff and volunteers tasted how God could change our lives and the lives of those in our ministry by shifting the way we approached our current paradigm, *nothing was off-limits*. We began to dream of more. In fact, together we penned these words to encourage ourselves not to give up or lose hope in the "in-between time"—the time between our envisioned future and our present reality:

We envision a new generation that will:

- Worship from the inside out, compelled by the Spirit—not through mandated behavior. They will worship as a lifestyle instead of as a moment or event.
- Possess a kingdom community mind-set and choose to usher in the realities of justice, mercy, love, the presence of God, forgiveness, humility, and service to life in everyday situations.
- Live with a global awareness, feel responsible for their brothers and sisters around the world, and

be compelled to make Christ known to every corner of the globe within their lifetime.

- Be knowledgeable about God's Word, but even more, through it will come to know God personally. They will investigate the Scriptures for themselves and will conclude that God's Word is Truth and will be unashamed of it.

- Know God's voice, desire to obey it, and then obey it in and through the power of the Holy Spirit as they depend on Him alone for strength.

Each of these statements became our marching orders. We prayerfully sought how God wanted us to respond to Him to create environments where we would need to give up "prime real estate" in our programming to allow God's Spirit to move. We asked Him to teach us how to make worship a lifestyle and culture and not just the singing portion of our services.

We considered in what practical ways we could allow the students in our ministry to feel that they were a part of God's kingdom in the here and now. We evaluated in what ways we provided opportunities for our students to flex their faith muscles—sharing the gospel with those who didn't yet know Jesus—and to sense both the calling and the responsibility on their lives to be His ambassadors to those people.

INVESTIGATING THE BIBLE

We searched every corner of our ministry plans, leaving no "sacred cow" free of scrutiny. And just when we thought we were done with our transformation, we sensed God asking us to look deeper into our curricula. This included the way we taught and represented God's Word, along with how and when we encouraged our youth to investigate the Bible for themselves.

Most of our students were not bringing their own Bibles to church, and it simply became easier to project Bible passages onto the large screens or allow them to use the Bible app on their smartphones. There is nothing wrong with either of these, and they can be helpful for many. But we wanted our students to actually hold Bibles in their hands, shuffle through the pages, become familiar with the layout, and have the satisfaction of finding the passages for themselves.

Further, we wanted them to read the Bible with fresh eyes of discovery, to see what came before in the context and what came after. We began to take the necessary steps to make sure every student had access to a Bible as well as to carve out time to allow for the process of finding the chapter and verse being taught.

TIME TO LISTEN

Of course we said we wanted the students in our ministry to hear God's voice as their primary teacher, but we had to ask the deafening question of whether we had allocated the time and space for them to do just that. When you are programming a service, every minute is precious.

Would we be willing to give up this prime real estate for "listening" when so many other things demanded those minutes? We had to. If we believed the things we were saying, we *had* to.

And so it began. After our time in God's Word, there was a time to sit quietly and listen and then respond to God. Those were humble days, filled with excitement and even some regret.

On one Sunday, God's Spirit decided to take us to the next level. A first grader announced during storytelling time that God had convicted him to give away much of what had been accumulating in his closet and drawers. He confessed before his peers that he had been hoarding, unwilling to share with those less fortunate. After sharing, he confidently took his seat among his peers, and no one moved for what seemed like eternity. Then, someone else stood.

A third-grade girl shared that God had been speaking to her, telling her that He wanted her to take better care of her body. He wanted her to be healthy so she could be all He wanted her to be in His Big Story.

And the stories continued: a middle school boy was prompted to forgive his unfaithful father; a high school girl wanted to be bold on her non-Christian campus; and another student wanted his dad to know Jesus.

During this moment of "pause" that we had carved out, students were hearing from the almighty God. His Spirit was moving, and none of us had ever seen anything like it.

Of course it didn't happen overnight. It wasn't even formulaic. We knew this was true because just a few weeks later, in many respects, the sacredness of the former service was lacking that particular morning. But we were all eyewitnesses that it *did* happen once, and if it could happen once, it could happen again. We could all testify that God had shown up and moved supernaturally in the lives of those in our ministry, teaching them how to worship.

THE SPIRIT TEACHES US TO WORSHIP

There are seventeen different words in the Bible, in both Hebrew and Greek, that represent the idea of worship. Many of the words that are translated as "worship" in English are related to the nuances of worship, such as glory, honor, reverence, awe, service, beauty, and holiness.

The complexity of the word is perhaps due in part to the majesty of God Himself. How could one word contain the grandeur and depth of our God? Ironically, we find ourselves so often using this word to describe merely the singing portion of our weekend services.

Technically speaking, singing is not worship. Singing is a *means* to worship. Worship is the act of ascribing worth or value to another. Paul spoke of another way to worship when he said that offering our bodies as living sacrifices—all that we do and say—is our spiritual act of service (Rom. 12:1–2).

The word for service in the original language is *latreia*, which can also be translated as "worship." To serve is an act of worship, or a *means* to worship. Kneeling, bowing, and falling prostrate on one's face are also means to worship.

There are many *means* to worship, but worship occurs only when it is from the heart. To sing may or may not be worshipful; it depends on the heart. To bow may or may not be worshipful; it depends on the heart. And to serve may or may not be worshipful—it too depends on what is in the heart. Is this act or deed motivated by awe, love, fascination, fear, or the grace of God? When it is, our God deems it true worship.

A HEART'S RESPONSE

Perhaps this is why Jesus said to His disciples, "If you love me, keep my commands" (John 14:15). He set up obedience as an act of (or means to) worship; it is worship from a heart of *response*. In this case, it is a heart responding out of love.

The woman caught in the very act of adultery was forgiven by Christ and sent on her way. Jesus told her, "Go, and … sin no more" (John 8:11 ESV). Her new life would be a worshipful response to God's forgiveness. True worship always comes from a heart that is *responding to God*.

In Exodus 15, when God led the Israelites across the dry ground of the Red Sea, His people responded by singing songs to Him. In 1 Samuel 7, when God was faithful to deliver His people in battle, Samuel stopped to respond by setting up the Ebenezer stone. Look at the people in Acts who witnessed the day of Pentecost. After the Spirit descended upon them, they responded as a community by sharing everything they had for the cause of Christ. Worship is our response to God's power and glory. It's our response to who He is.

AUTHENTIC VULNERABILITY

Jeff, a friend of ours, mentors young worship leaders. He is tenacious about making sure they know they are neither performers nor simply musicians. To lead worship means to usher people into the presence of God's glory—to allow them to see His holiness, goodness, and love so they can respond to *that*.

Jeff once said that authentic worship brings authentic vulnerability, and authentic vulnerability brings authentic worship. The two are inseparable. We cannot worship God with pride or pretense, and in true worship God gently breaks down our defenses. Jeff added, "We also respond to God in worship because He subjected Himself to the utmost vulnerability by becoming flesh and dying upon a cross."

When children are young, they are by nature very vulnerable. They are willing to "say it as it is." This must be beautiful worship to God. With pure hearts, they teach us what our heavenly Father is looking for. But something happens when those children get older. As they hit puberty, they are suddenly concerned with what others think. That concern begins to take up the primary space in their hearts, and worship is tainted as a result.

But what could happen if we began to cultivate deeper worship opportunities when our children are young, so that when they are older they care more about their relationship with God than those around them?

CREATING SPACE TO ENCOUNTER GOD'S SPIRIT

Consider these questions as you envision a new generation of worshippers:

- What could it look like to allow our students to pause to listen to God?
- In what ways can we give our students options in how they feel led to respond to God?

- How can we create a place for our students to write out their prayers and praises?
- Where can we carve out time for a young generation to stand up and declare God's goodness and faithfulness and to celebrate that bold expression?

Tommy, a family ministry leader who was on my (Michelle's) ministry staff when we first began to implement a time of worship response after the Bible-teaching portion of our service for children and youth, recounted how those early days felt for us as leaders:

> I remember the fear I had going into that service. We wanted silence for a few moments after the message to ask the students to think about God and then to declare one of God's attributes out loud, finishing the phrase "God is …" But we had never allowed for that kind of time before, and we had instructed our staff and leaders *not* to lead by example.
>
> We wanted the Holy Spirit to be the teacher in that time and space. Stepping back was a huge step of faith for us. We told ourselves that no matter how long the silence was once we set the stage, we would not jump in and fill that silence with our own voices. We knew it would be difficult to resist the urge to jump in, but I don't think we were prepared for the level of difficulty we experienced.
>
> A couple of us stood in the back while the worship leader said, "Let's stop for a moment and think

about the amazing characteristics of God. Who is He? What's one word that comes to mind when you think of Him? Who would like to share?" Our students were generally "chatty," but at that time, asking them to speak in a group was, to them, uncomfortable and scary.

We might as well have asked them each to sing a solo for all of us! So there we were, sitting with fifty students … in silence. Waiting … waiting. Nothing happened.

Our team sat in the uncomfortable silence, desperately wanting to fix it. But instead we continued to wait and pray. We prayed that the Holy Spirit would lead and teach during this time and prompt kids to stand and declare God's goodness.

Then, out of nowhere, one girl cautiously stood up, hunched over and staring at the ground, and said sheepishly, "God … is … amazing." From there another student stood up and declared, "God is powerful." Then another and another.

Suddenly, without any adult leader, the students began to stand and not just say words, but *shout* them—over one another! In that moment we realized the power the Holy Spirit has to speak, nudge, and guide us all. We also realized that worship doesn't just happen in a song and that God can be glorified by declaring one simple word.

This illustrates a few very important aspects of worship as response. First, there was a conviction that God did and would speak to young people. Second, we were committed to wait on God no matter what happened. We all literally had to put our faith on the line with anticipation that if God didn't show up and prompt a young person to speak, then nothing else was going to happen that day. And finally, there was a simplicity to this form of worship. There were no cool band members, no special effects, no bells and whistles—just simple words ascribing worth to God. *Worship*.

WORSHIP BEYOND SUNDAY

One parent shared with me at church that earlier in the week she was having a sad moment because of a conflict with a neighbor. Her daughter saw her teary eyed and came close. This little girl then said to her mom, "Let's take a moment and listen for God's voice." They did take a moment to listen for God's voice, and this time of stillness lifted the mother's spirits. She said she knew that her daughter had learned that expression from the church's ministry on the weekend, and now she had wanted to create that kind of space in their home!

Where in modern culture do children and their parents have the opportunity simply to be still?

Psalm 46:10 says, "Be still, and know that I am God." I love that in the stillness there is knowledge of God. It is not stillness or quietness for the sake of just being still; rather, it is for the sake of knowing God.

Do we desperately need to know Him? His voice? His love? His peace? Yes … we desperately do!

Think of the families in your church. The crazy, hectic lives they are leading constantly drive them away from knowing the depths of God's character and His peace. Since worship is a response to who God is by listening to His Spirit, it's more difficult than ever to truly worship with our current agendas. So when we consider the family events we might plan, we cannot neglect the fact that families need an opportunity "to be still" just as much as they need to be entertained or have fun together.

There are many other ways families can consider living lives of worshipful response after hearing from and being taught by God's Spirit. However, the difference is that they are not doing these things in order to be "good Christians." Rather, they choose to do these things with a heart of response that cannot be contained.

Remember King David, who broke out dancing in the streets because his gratitude to God couldn't be contained? Today's youth are in the best position to have uninhibited lives of worship, so let's create places in our homes and weekend services where they can respond to His love and goodness without the barriers that our structures sometimes impose. We have the privilege of allowing God to teach and proclaim Himself in every way. Let's become faith communities that place God's Spirit in His proper place—and do so more intentionally than ever before.

MINISTRY ASSESSMENT

Take time to reflect, respond, and dream about how God might use the concept of listening to Him in your life personally or in your ministry to children, students, and their families.

Listen

After reading about the Holy Spirit's role as the teacher of transformation and empowerment, where do you feel you may have neglected to put up a sail to catch the wind of how He is moving in your ministry? In what ways have you perhaps motored your way in your own direction or at your own speed in your personal spiritual life or in your ministry? In what ways has God's Spirit convicted you as you have been awakened afresh to His purposes?

So What?

Take some time to respond to God based on the things He has revealed to you in reading this chapter. Is this a time of repentance and humility? Is this a time to seek wisdom and guidance? Is this a time for creative anticipation and ideating? However God's Spirit is speaking to you right now, respond to Him with petition and thanksgiving.

Now What?

Next, what dreams has God inspired in you for the children, youth, and their families in your ministry? If you were to write your own dream statements of an envisioned generation, what statements would come to mind? Write them down and keep them as inspirational beacons while on your journey.

If you want to be encouraged by how others have been inspired to put these things into practice both in the church and in the homes of those in our ministries, read these real-life ministry examples:

1. Parent Prayer Stations

Dawn Heckert is a family pastor in Kansas. This past year she offered an eight-week Spiritual Parenting class. On seven of the nights when the class met, she did the normal training; but on one night, without the parents' knowledge, she decided to do something completely different. Instead of providing the normal DVD clips, teaching, and table discussions, she turned the room into a prayer experience.

The room was dimly lit and had different stations at which to consider God, His faithfulness, their children, and their roles as parents. There were intentional places to read and meditate on Scripture verses pertaining to these subjects as well. The night was not what the parents may have *wanted*—they wanted information on how to parent their children—but it was what they *needed*. They needed to be still with God. He spoke. They listened. They spoke. God heard their prayers. God comforted, healed, and encouraged. God was worshipped that night in their responses to Him and in the days that followed in their homes.

2. Conversation Starters in the Home

Often parents want spiritual conversations with their children, but they don't know how to enter into them. Angelina Pavone, a preschool director in California, helps her students' parents do this by asking "wonder" questions. Here are a few examples:

- I wonder … how do you think God can talk to you?
- I wonder … how did God put all of the stars in the sky?
- I wonder … how does God pay special attention to everyone in the world?
- I wonder … how do you know that God is with you?
- I wonder … what special thing does God love about you?
- I wonder … how does God show you His love?
- I wonder … what do you think God might want to say to you?

As the child responds, parents have an opportunity to respond also. When finished, a parent can simply say, "What can we tell God right now about how we feel?" As the child answers, that statement alone can be a response of worship, and the parent can say, "Your answer is a gift of worship to God." Or the parent and child can verbalize the worship into a prayer as well.

For older kids and teenage students, sometimes a "finish the sentence" is a great way to generate a conversation about spiritual matters without forcing a "correct" answer. Such statements might include:

- If I could be more like Jesus in one way, it would be …
- The best time I ever had helping someone else was when I …
- I feel closest to God when …

- When I pray to God, I feel …
- Sometimes I can feel that God wants me to do something because …
- I know for sure that my prayer was answered when I prayed for …
- If I could be known for one thing it would be …
- I think God hears my prayers because …

3. Physical Markers

Parents can pray as a response to each of the thoughts that are conveyed in the above conversations. Also, sometimes creating a physical marker is a great way for older students to worship. For example, Pastor Alex Douglas near Toronto, Canada, encourages families to have a jar of smooth stones with a permanent marker nearby. When a family member wants to celebrate something about God, he or she can write it on a stone and put the stone back in the jar. When the jar is full of written-on stones, the family can create mosaic stepping-stones for the yard and begin another jar of stones to remember God's character in worship.

4. Prayer Walls

To provide a physical space where prayer is made prominent in the home is a tangible way to allow families to worship together. Some families I know have whiteboards or chalkboards and can write prayers to God for thanksgiving and praise. Others take wooden picture frames (without the glass) and string twine around and inside them in different directions, creating a web. Then, with small pieces of paper and clothespins nearby, family members can write their prayers and attach them to the twine.

If you want to see examples of how to make these for your ministry, visit: truministry.com/worshipresponsestations.

5. God Is ...

Having a place simply to declare who God is can be one of the most tangible acts of worship. As we ascribe to Him the qualities that only He is, we declare He alone is God.

Several families from a church in Omaha, Nebraska, have painted statements of God on a large rock outside their houses or have chalkboards dedicated to this in their homes.

Recently, in my own home, we had words that described God's character posted on our refrigerator. Often as we were making dinner, I would ask my children, "Which one of these words stands out to you today, and why?" Their answers often led us down the paths of what they were thinking, but their responses also led our time of worship in prayer or thanksgiving at dinner.

6

ESSENTIAL FIVE: GOD'S GRAND REDEMPTIVE NARRATIVE

It's Not about You … but Your Part Is Significant

> *At the heart of our Christian faith is a story.… Unless the story is known, understood, owned, and lived, we and our children will not have Christian faith.*[1]
>
> John H. Westerhoff

I remember being compelled as a young adult by the grand meta-narrative of Scripture. After being raised in a Christian home and a Bible-teaching church, I finally had the ultimate "Aha!" moment when I discovered that the Bible was not just a collection of Sunday school stories about the good guys and the bad guys but rather a continuous epic story line of a loving God redeeming all of creation back into right relationship with Himself.

One story. One main character. One God loving me.

IT'S REALLY TRUE

And it's a true story! There's a small church in Southern California that meets in a nightclub and holds children's church in the green room. This unique church venue reflects the passion of the pastor to reach people who wouldn't normally come to a traditional service. The church service is filled mostly with brand-new Christians. And because the parents are brand-new Christians, the kids are brand-new Christians, and the Big God Story is completely new to all of them.

In the nightclub's green room, my friend Debbie had been telling the Big God Story from the beginning—relating to the kids how God promised to send the Redeemer who would restore our relationships with God. Over many months, she unfolded for them how the promised Redeemer—Jesus—was eventually born as a baby, lived a sinless life, and then died for our sins.

One day, when it was pouring rain outside, a little girl sat listening as my friend told the part of the Big God Story when Jesus was born in the little suburb of Bethlehem. The little girl heard about the angels singing and the shepherds running to worship the newborn King. Her eyes grew bigger and bigger as she listened. Then she interrupted, asking with skepticism in her voice, "Is this true?"

"Yes!" my friend replied enthusiastically. "It's really true!" The little girl's jaw dropped open wide enough to reveal her tiny molars.

As my friend continued to read, the little girl sat in shock. Then she interrupted again, "Is this *really* true? Are you sure?"

"Yes!" my friend replied. "It's *really* true."

Because we've heard the story so many times, we might be tempted to gloss over the amazement that it's all really true. God *really* did promise to send the Redeemer, He *really* kept the promise alive throughout history, He *really* sent His Son to die for us, and He *really* did redeem us from our sin, because He *really* loves us that much!

The Big God Story is amazing—and true! And sometimes it takes a new believer, a child, to remind us how shocking it is.

THE MAIN CHARACTER

We often tell fragmented stories of God, Jesus, or other characters in the Bible, and we do so in ways that aren't linear. Even many young people who know the stories of the Bible can't tell you whether Abraham was born before David or if baby Jesus was alive when baby Moses was.

Stories told in isolation don't tell the bigger story in which God is central. Instead, baby Moses is the key figure one day, Noah is the key figure one day, and Jesus is merely the key figure on another occasion.

But by putting each story in the context of the main story, we can begin to elevate God, the Redeemer, to His rightful place in the story line—the main character. Perhaps you have had the privilege of hearing this grand story chronologically, but whether this is your first time or your hundredth time, sit back and enjoy it afresh. Let God reveal Himself and His redemption to you once again.

THE GRAND REDEMPTIVE NARRATIVE

God's story began in a beautiful garden nestled between four grand rivers. God created this garden and named it Eden. He made Adam and Eve to be in relationship with Him and to live in this beautiful garden together along with all of His creation. Unfortunately, Adam and Eve chose to sin against God and disobey His plans for them. Therefore, God told them to leave the garden and the intimate relationship they once shared with Him. This is referred to as the fall of Adam and Eve. But in the midst of this tragedy, God promised that one day a Redeemer would come. The promised Redeemer would save humankind from sin and, ultimately, the spiritual death that is the consequence of this sin. And so, humankind began to wait in expectation for the promise to be fulfilled.

Within just ten generations, the world had become so evil that God decided to destroy all humankind, except for Noah and his family, through a global flood. After the water subsided, Noah's family began to repopulate the earth, and nations were birthed from each of Noah's three sons. The nation of Israel would eventually rise from Noah's son Shem.

God gave a unique promise to a descendant of Shem named Abraham. This promise was that, through Abraham's son, God would set apart a nation that would demonstrate the relationship between God and humankind. As other nations saw this love relationship, they, too, would want to know the one true God. God also told Abraham that the promised Redeemer would be born out of his family line. This chosen nation would eventually be called Israel.

Abraham and his wife, Sarah, could not have children, so they began to doubt God's promise. Over time, they grew weary of waiting for God's timing and decided to "help God out" by having a son through their maidservant Hagar. This son was named Ishmael, and his descendants would become the Arab nations. However, twenty-five years after God promised Abraham and Sarah a son, the promised son, Isaac, was born.

Isaac had a son named Jacob. After Jacob wrestled with the angel of the Lord in a dream, God changed Jacob's name to Israel, which means "one who strives with God." Jacob had twelve sons, and the descendants of these twelve sons eventually became the twelve tribes of the land of Israel.

One of Jacob's sons, Joseph, was sold into slavery by his brothers and taken to Egypt. There, God allowed Joseph to rise to power under the pharaoh. Eventually, Jacob's entire family moved to Egypt. Joseph was able to keep them alive during seven years of famine in the region and, by doing so, preserved the family of the promise.

From Slavery to Freedom—Over and Over

After several centuries in Egypt, the descendants of Jacob (or Israel) became a large group of people called the Israelites. The Egyptians enslaved them, and the Israelites cried out to God for a redeemer. God chose an Israelite named Moses to lead his people out of Egypt and into the Promised Land so that they could worship God alone.

However, because of their disobedience and grumblings, that generation of Israelites spent the next forty years wandering in the desert between Egypt and the Promised Land. A new generation grew up in the wilderness with a respect for God and His power. This generation had grown up not being seduced by the powers of thousands of Egyptian gods, but rather seeing the work of the one and only true God daily in the provision of food, water, and guidance.

In fact, the only food they had ever eaten—manna—was supplied each day by God Himself. God guided this generation in the form of a pillar of cloud by day and a pillar of fire by night, so this new generation grew to know and trust Him alone. Joshua was the anointed leader of this young generation, and he led them to conquer the Promised Land God had set aside for His people.

Through years of battle, the Israelites claimed their land and settled down to raise families. (Today this is the nation of Israel, which occupies the land east of the Mediterranean Sea and northeast of Egypt.)

The Israelites, discontent because they were different from other nations, cried out for God to give them a king so they could be like other people. God's answer was no. Unhappy with His answer, the Israelites disobeyed and wandered away from Him, so God raised up other nations to bring punishment for their sins. When the nation of Israel repented, God sent leaders called judges to help them prevail against their enemies, and for a time they remained faithful to God. But soon they returned to their wicked ways, until calamity struck again.

This cycle of sin, suffering, repentance, and deliverance happened over and over, and Israel had many judges. The time of the judges, which included Gideon, Deborah, Samson, and Samuel, lasted more than 450 years.

Kings, Good and Bad

Despite God's warning that kings would take the people's money through taxes, their daughters as wives and slaves, and their sons to war, the people insisted on electing a king. Israel became a monarchy, and God was no longer her only King.

Saul was first to reign as king, but God quickly rejected him because of his pride and disobedience. David, a young shepherd who knew and loved God, followed as the second king. He sometimes sinned badly, but he remained "a man after God's heart" because he was humble and had a heart of worship. David's son Solomon became the third and final king of the united twelve tribes of Israel.

After Solomon's son became king, he faced rebellion in the land, and Israel split into two nations: ten tribes in the north (Israel) and two tribes in the south (Judah). The line of the promised Redeemer now followed the tribe of Judah in the south.

Israel (the ten tribes in the north) had only evil kings who led their people into great sin. Israel was eventually taken captive by Assyria, even after many prophets pleaded with the people to repent.

Although Judah (the two tribes in the south) had a few good kings and even several revivals, they, too, disobeyed God over and over until He finally let the Babylonian Empire conquer them. The city of Jerusalem, the center of God's people, was utterly destroyed. The Babylonians took the people of Judah away into captivity.

The Jews in Captivity

Some of the Jews (people of Judah) kept their faith in God alive even during their captivity in Babylon. We know of Daniel and his righteous acts of prayer in the midst of hungry lions. We know how Shadrach, Meshach, and Abednego stood strong in the face of pressure to compromise.

Eventually, Babylon fell to the Persian Empire. Then a Jewish orphan named Esther became the queen of Persia, and God strategically worked through her to save her people from death. Also under Persian rule, Nehemiah (a Jewish cupbearer for the Persian king Artaxerxes) returned to Israel to rebuild Jerusalem's walls. The Persian king not only let this happen, but he paid for it too! In all, one of the greatest construction projects of the ancient world was completed in a mere forty-nine days, even in the midst of great opposition in the land. The lineage of the promised Christ was now back in the motherland of Israel, and the Old Testament came to a close.

Then something strange happened: God was silent. He didn't speak through a prophet, a priest, or a king. The promise was alive, but it was hidden and still. The people waited for the promise to be revealed. Nearly four hundred years passed before the opening words in the New Testament.

The Redeemer Arrives at Last

The lineage recorded for us by Matthew and Luke shows that the same promise that began in the garden remained true throughout thousands of years. Despite Satan's efforts to eliminate the people of

God, they prevailed. And at the appointed time in history that had been prophesied hundreds of years before, the Redeemer arrived in an obscure town called Bethlehem.

Jesus was born. He was the Messiah promised in Genesis, predicted throughout history, and finally He was here on earth in the flesh.

He was born of a virgin, Mary, who raised him with her eventual husband, Joseph, in the town of Nazareth. Jesus grew in wisdom and stature and in favor with God and humankind.

When Jesus was grown, His cousin John the Baptist became a voice in the wilderness preparing the way for Jesus the Messiah's ministry. Soon after, Jesus called Peter, James, John, and the remainder of the twelve disciples. He ministered to the poor, healed the sick, raised the dead, and redeemed the outcasts. Jesus lived and proclaimed the kingdom of God, demonstrated His divine power over creation, and taught His disciples and the world a radical new way to live.

He became a man for the purpose of being the perfect sacrifice who would pay the price for our sins. The Jewish people practiced animal sacrifice as the price for sin. They made offerings of pure, undefiled lambs for the sins they committed against God, just as God had commanded them in the Law of Moses.

Jesus became the once-and-for-all sacrifice who gives every man, woman, and child access to God for all time. He was the final sacrificial Lamb of God who satisfied God's justice for all time, for everyone who accepts it.

Jesus's death provided the way for our sins to be forgiven. His resurrection cleared the way for victory over death. His ascension into heaven enabled Him to send the Holy Spirit to abide in us. And

His Spirit empowers the church to live out the message of salvation. The book of Acts tells how the Spirit did this in the earliest church in Jerusalem and in the apostle Paul's missionary journeys.

Today the Holy Spirit continues to work in each of our lives for the glory of God, allowing each one of us to be a part of His Big Story until He returns.

He's Coming Back!

The story doesn't end with us, though; it is much bigger than that! Jesus will return. He will return not shrouded by humanness but completely unveiled in all of His glory. He will ride in victory on His white horse to proclaim that He is King of Kings and Lord of Lords forever.

He will judge the nations and eventually send Satan and his followers to an eternity of suffering and separation. Those who love God and who have accepted His Son, Jesus, will live with Him in the new heaven and new earth forever, in relationship with God—the way it all began in the garden. The way it *should* be. And from that day on, for all of eternity, we will be with the promised Lord and Redeemer forever and ever. Amen!

INFORMATION AND TRANSFORMATION

After being impacted by both the simplicity and magnificence of this story of God, I (Michelle) found myself surprised that we taught isolated Bible *stories* to our children and youth with little or no context to the whole. I became concerned about the danger of merely transmitting *biblical information* within what Randy Frazee called "the Lower Story."[2] These are the stories of individual people in the Bible such as Noah, David, Ruth, or Paul—yet without *transformation* from "the Upper Story" of redemption and relationship.

So that's when I decided I wanted to try something new in our approach to both our children's and student ministries. I decided to teach God's Word as *one* story line, as well as to teach it chronologically, to our elementary students.

Of course this would present some apparent problems. If we began teaching creation (Genesis) in the fall quarter, we wouldn't be able to get through the entire Old Testament before December, when Jesus was to be born at Christmas (at least in the church calendar).

On top of this, we wouldn't be able to align Easter (and its ever-changing dates) on schedule with His death and resurrection and still have enough of the New Testament to take us through the remainder of spring and all of summer. As children's ministry practitioners, many of us have always lived in the world of "scope and sequence" and church holidays, right? This idea to veer from that just seemed absurd.

Yet after considering the multitude of problems that might arise from teaching the Bible as a chronological narrative, I decided to take the plunge anyway. I wondered if what we would *gain* from telling God's Story as it was intended would be worth the inconveniences.

One of our solutions was to tell about the birth of Christ in the winter through the perspective of Old Testament prophecy, and we could pause on Easter to simply tell the entire Big God Story with an emphasis on His death and resurrection. After only nine months into our pilot study of this methodology, one elementary boy became impatient—*in a good way.*

RELATIONSHIP BIRTHED OUT OF CONTEXT

You see, when you teach the Bible as one story and not a collection of stories, there is a natural cliffhanger moment every week. It's a continuing story line, and the idea of coming back next week to hear what *happens next* is naturally woven into the text.

One week, a boy went home on a mission; he couldn't take the suspense any longer. He took out his young readers Bible (a condensed version of the actual text) and read it from start to finish. Then, when Sunday arrived, he burst through the classroom doors and called for everyone's attention. "All right, everyone," he shouted, "I went home, I read the whole thing … and we're all going to be okay.… Jesus is coming back!"

In over twenty years of ministry to children at that point, I had never heard of a child motivated to read the whole book in one week because he was so captivated by the story! I realized that in the past I had inadvertently made the story *so small.* Paul and Silas got out of jail, Daniel was not eaten by the ravenous lions, and Ruth and Boaz lived happily ever after. There was no need to find out what happened *next.*

Furthermore, in our ministries to youth, although we wanted to teach relevant topics and do so within sermon series, we began to always launch a series within the context of the grand narrative. We would give a short overview for those who needed a quick reminder or simply to be sensitive to those who joined us having not been part of a children's ministry or a Christian home.

On Easter and other designated weekends, we started to set aside the teaching time to tell the entire biblical story from beginning to end in creative ways. Soon, we found that our youth could often tell the "story" better than most adults could! But even greater, we witnessed vital personal relationships with God being birthed out of telling His story with Him at the center of that story. Somehow, this small contextual adjustment made the information so much more transforming to our students.

DANGEROUS LIE

Sometimes I am tempted to believe that *I* am the main character, that the story is really about *me*—because after all, *I am in every scene*. But that's a lie. It's a lie children and students are told on every TV channel, on every social media site, and in every song. Sometimes it's blatant and sometimes subtle, but nonetheless, today's youth are being made to believe that the greatest story ever told is happening in their obscure little worlds.

Can you see how dangerous Satan's lie is? If he can get me to believe that this life is a story centered on me and my happiness, then I will see life as a series of events that allow me either to succeed or to fail in this endeavor.

I begin to manipulate people and events to my own benefit. After all, don't we always want the main character to be victorious in the end? We want her to succeed and be happy. Thus, my happiness becomes primary.

The problem with this perspective is that life is sometimes hard and unfair. I can't always control life, events, and other people. Then what? And even when I do manage to control people, that's not what I or they were created for. In using them to make my life work, I bring them harm.

If children and youth consistently hear the grand redemptive narrative, both in our ministries and in their homes, they will have the privilege of catching a glimpse of the wonder of it all.

There is wonderful mystery in who God is and how He has chosen a part for each of us to play. We can never play the role of the main character, but when we understand why we can't, we rest in the knowledge that we were never created to do so. When this happens, we are able to worship God and not ourselves. We are free to be who we were created to be: true worshippers in every aspect of our lives.

This is, after all, the goal of ministry to families, right? To help each member of that family live a life of worship. I love how the apostle Paul said this in Romans 12:1–2:

> So here's what I want you to do, God helping you: Take your everyday, ordinary life—your sleeping, eating, going-to-work, and walking-around life— and place it before God as an offering. Embracing what God does for you is the best thing you can do for him. Don't become so well-adjusted to your culture that you fit into it without even thinking. Instead, fix your attention on God. You'll be changed from the inside out. Readily recognize what he wants from you, and quickly respond to

it. Unlike the culture around you, always dragging you down to its level of immaturity, God brings the best out of you, develops well-formed maturity in you. (MSG)

IMPACT AND INFLUENCE

Hearing God's epic story profoundly influenced one student who had been in our ministry for several years. He had heard this narrative of redemption each week and learned that he could have a part in that story. The fact that God had him in mind for a role when God wrote the story inspired him. This thought followed him as he graduated out of our children's ministry and entered middle school.

Not long after his transition, I received an invitation from him to join a Facebook group. It was titled "God has a Big Story, and you can be a part of it." Wow! He actually heard what we were saying, and he grasped that God was inviting him into it.

The next weekend I asked him what had motivated him to create such a group. He said he was amazed that every day at school he could sense that his peers were living their lives aimlessly or without knowledge that something *bigger* was going on around them. He was saddened that they neither knew that God was writing an amazing story nor were aware that they were invited into it by His grace and love.

This young man's plan seemed simple: He would post blog updates after each week at church, recounting what he had learned from the grand redemptive narrative, and then ask questions that would provoke others to consider how they might play parts in it.

Here was a middle schooler who had been eternally impacted by the *story* in such a profound way that he could not help but live out the gospel.

That's the essence of God's Story. Good and evil war with each other, evil seems to overtake the world, but then Jesus shows up and brings justice, and we who know Him are saved. He makes everything good, and those who follow Jesus all win in the end! I don't know about you, but I want to be part of *that* story, and I definitely want to be on the winning side. I want to be one of Jesus's friends when He shows up on the scene, and I want Satan to be punished!

This is a story young people can relate to, and yet so often we allow them to see only pieces of it at any given time. When we do that, we prevent them from experiencing the power of living it and sharing it.

WHAT STORY ARE WE LIVING?

We are designed to love stories and to live stories. We all live inside a story, whether we recognize it or not. We tell ourselves a story of what the world is about, what is important, and what *our place* in the story is.

Yet our culture bombards our children and students with a counterfeit story that says life is "all about me." It tells them that they are born by chance, that life is about getting what they want and being happy, and that death is the end of the story.

The Bible tells a different story—an epic story of the Father pursuing His children in order to have a personal relationship with each one of them.

This story is "all about God."

It tells children and youth that they are born because God wants them and made them in His image, that life is about knowing and loving Him, and that death is *not at all* the end of the story.

It tells them that the grand redemptive narrative has been lived by people for many centuries. In it, God is taking us on an exciting and unpredictable journey. He has a script for each one of us to play, and this story line is completely centered on Jesus, our Messiah.

During our childhood and teenage years, our world is very small. We see *everything* from our vantage points and how it affects us directly or indirectly. It's only as we mature that we begin to see the world as much more complex and we begin to see our role was designed to be one of a servant—first submitting to the will and plans of our King as well as addressing the needs of those around us.

THE STORY ISN'T OVER

Matthew 1 and Luke 2 recount the genealogy of Jesus Christ. If you read these records, they reveal the men and women Jesus was related to: Abraham, Isaac, Jacob, Ruth, Jesse, David, Solomon, Ahaz, Hezekiah, Josiah, Rahab, and Tamar—men and women we hear about throughout the Big God Story!

Often, we skip over genealogies because we think they have no personal application. But since I now know "the story" that God was telling through these lives, I am astounded. Throughout this narrative, God was strategically setting up people, events, and situations in order to proclaim the promise given to us in the birth, death, and resurrection of Christ—the promised Redeemer. Everyone has a very specific part and purpose. Whether they fall during an important scene, fumble their lines, or exit stage left when it should have been right, God's purpose and plan remain unthwarted.

Throughout God's grand redemptive story we see the thread of love, grace, long-suffering, and holiness from the Author of the story—God Himself. We find startling revelations, seasons of pain or separation, joyful surprises, and answers to long-awaited prayers. We see the ups and downs of relationships, the turmoil in trial, and the provision of our heavenly Father. We are impacted by His redemption and immeasurable love despite our fear and failures.

When reading God's Word as one continuous narrative, or even one story in the context of such a story line, we begin to discover that this is not a story that merely takes place in the past, but rather one that we are in the very midst of—*today*.

This story isn't over!

God is using us, just as He used Moses, Deborah, Jeremiah, and Mary. He is offering us (and each family in our ministries) a place in His story to further His kingdom until its ultimate fulfillment. We sometimes get so distracted by today's script that we forget the purpose of the story altogether—that when Jesus returns in all His glory, He will usher His children into an eternal and personal relationship with Him, free from sin and separation.

We are living and breathing testaments of His redemptive plan. In the same way we have seen God's plan accomplished through the lives of Abraham, Esther, and Joseph, retrospectively, it's thrilling to think that someday we will see how *our* lives have built upon the lives of other believers to further and proclaim God's story of redemption.

THE GOSPEL

The word *gospel* in the New Testament can be translated "good news." The original Greek word is *euaggelion*. By definition, this word proclaims the good news of the coming Messiah, but it also refers to the Giver of the Messiah, the plans leading up to His coming, and the condition for which the Messiah was needed in the first place. The good news is the *entire* story!

In the past, I have erroneously compartmentalized the gospel to exclusively mean the part where Jesus paid the price for my sin. Jesus commissioned us to spread the good news, but if we misunderstand the message as an isolated event, then we will be story bearers of that alone. If we understand the charge to spread the entire story line, then we will need to be prepared to tell it *all*!

The first step in preparing ourselves and the families of this generation to be evangelists of the good news will be to *know* it. Then, as we know the story, we need opportunities to *tell* the story. I've come to realize that we need to practice telling the story.

SELLING OR STORYTELLING?

When we say the word *practice* in the context of evangelizing, many of us may groan, thinking of the multitude of verses and points we need to memorize and rehearse. Evangelizing has often gotten a bad rap in churches, as well as among the unchurched, simply because it can feel like a sales pitch. Just when our listener feels that he or she may have eluded the sell, we begin our up-sell strategy, fearing we will lose another one.

But what if a new generation, compelled by the metanarrative of Scripture, simply became storytellers? What if the story, so embedded in their hearts and lives, organically manifested itself in winsome prose and verse in everyday situations?

We have been given the gift of teaching a new generation the bigness of God's story while allowing them to find their small places in it. As they do, sharing these two things can become as natural for them as sharing their statuses on Facebook. It's not a speech they need to memorize, but rather a story they get to live—live out loud in the simplest of terms.

Max Lucado once simplified the bigness of the gospel down to this:

> You come before the judgment seat of God full of rebellion and mistakes. Because of his justice he cannot dismiss your sin, but because of his love he cannot dismiss you. So in an act that stunned the heavens, he punished himself on the cross for your sins. God's justice and love are equally honored. And you, God's creation, are forgiven.[3]

Wow! That is a gripping rendition of the gospel, and it takes only twenty seconds to share!

BEING A PART OF THE BIG STORY

When we embarked on this journey of knowing and telling the gospel, we had to brainstorm practical ways to make God's redemptive narrative come to life for our students and their families. We wanted them to grasp the hugeness of the narrative yet simplify it for children as young as preschool age.

In one of my (Michelle's) first attempts to share the story in its totality with our elementary students, I simply printed on paper the names of individuals and places recorded in poignant moments throughout biblical history. Such people and places included creation, Adam and Eve, Noah, Abraham, Isaac, Jacob, Judah, Joseph, Egypt, Moses, Joshua, the Promised Land, the crucifixion and resurrection, and so on. There was one special piece of paper that was a different color. It was entitled "The Promise."

Then I began to tell God's story. I started with Adam and Eve in the garden, choosing two kids to come up front and hold their corresponding characters' names. I told about how God had a perfect relationship with Adam and Eve and that He loved them. After I shared that Adam and Eve chose to disobey God, I talked about the consequences that He gave them and that they had to leave the garden. With this, I physically ushered the two children off the stage.

"But," I told the children, "God made a promise to them that one day a redeemer would come, and that redeemer would conquer sin and give us a perfect relationship with God again." I then picked one child to be the Promise.

I went on to select children from the audience to come up and hold particular characters' names or stand as places where those people traveled to or from—always identifying where the hope of the Promise was at any given time. The kids were captivated as I divided the room in two when the twelve tribes of Israel split into the ten tribes in the north (Israel) and the two tribes in the south (Judah). Then I asked where the Promise needed to be at this point. When they all shouted out, "Judah!" I realized they were finally getting it.

When Jesus was born, I turned the Promise's sign over to reveal the name Jesus. The kids had this visual to help them identify that the same promise made in the garden, prophesied and preserved throughout history, was and is Jesus the Messiah. This allowed them to see that the Old Testament and the New Testament are parts of one story line in which God always had in mind His remedy to bring us back to a perfect relationship with Him. And then, when Jesus died, the children understood why—and when He rose from the dead, they cheered!

Next, I invited them to be a part of this story today, helping them see that it is still being written in each one of our lives. This story will continue until Jesus, the Promise, comes again—and when He does, those who love Him and have accepted His gift of grace for their sin will live with Him in a perfect relationship forever and ever.

From that day on, we continued to seek other creative ways to reinforce the big narrative of God's redemption for every age group, from preschool through high school. We created a physical timeline on our wall where kids could see all of history at a glance. We had storytellers tell the story with pictures and other visuals that were attached to a clothesline as the story progressed. One leader told the story using upside-down cups to build a pyramid, showing how each event was tied to all the others. At the end, he gave each child a cup to write his or her name on and then add to the pyramid, showing that we too can be a part of this redemptive narrative.

LIVING TESTAMENTS

Once a child or student grasps the bigger story line, it's important to captivate each one into the part that God wants him or her to play in it. One church we know has a "storytelling wall" where students of all ages can tell how God has been writing their stories over the past week or weeks. The leader shared some of the story lines written by her students:

> God, I hear You.
>
> You have changed my heart forever.
>
> You are the provider we needed to pay our rent.
>
> God is healer.
>
> God's love changes everything in my life.
>
> I can't stop thinking about You, Jesus.
>
> I'm not alone.
>
> I matter.
>
> I've been washed clean.

These students are becoming *living testaments*.

Think about each of those statements. Wouldn't you love to hear those words from the mouth of a student in your ministry? Unrehearsed, this leader is giving her students the opportunity to *practice* being storytellers.

The entire faith community can read these words and testimonies. In doing so, these stories serve as a mosaic of encouragement to the rest of the church body.

Although it won't happen overnight, I believe this new generation, captivated by the gospel of redemption in the entirety of God's Word, has the best chance to reach our lost world and invite *everyone* in it to play *their* part for *His* glory.

MINISTRY ASSESSMENT

Take time to reflect, respond, and dream about how God might use His grand redemptive narrative in your life personally or in your ministry to children and their families.

Listen

After reading about God's grand narrative of redemption, how has its message had a fresh impact on you? In what areas did God's Spirit convict you as you considered how you have lived out your part in His story? Spend some time writing an account of your thoughts and reflections.

So What?

We have the most impact on the communities we lead when God's truths flow through us first. Take a few moments to respond to God about the following statements.

- God is Redeemer.
- God has invited you into His story through grace.
- You are not alone.
- You are free … *indeed.*
- Jesus is coming again.
- The good news is the entire story line.

Now What?

What dreams has God inspired in you for making His redemptive narrative come to life in your ministry? How might the things He revealed to you become catalysts to make some adjustments in your ministry to children/students *and their families*?

ESSENTIAL SIX: GOD IS CENTRAL

Fixing Our Focus

*A person will worship something, have no doubt about
that…. That which dominates our imaginations and
our thoughts will determine our lives, and our character.
Therefore, it behooves us to be careful what we worship,
for what we are worshipping we are becoming.*[1]

Ralph Waldo Emerson

Have you noticed that one thousand compliments plus one criticism equals one criticism in your mind? "The critic's math,"[2] as author Jon Acuff called it, happens when we put ourselves at the center of our lives, as though people's opinions of us matter most in determining our self-worth and satisfaction.

When I (Megan) put myself at my selfish epicenter, I spend an embarrassing amount of time and energy trying to make, have, do, or possess something, or simply just be noticed. And, even if I focus on others, it's to remind myself that *I matter*.

We do it all the time. We even adjust our smartphone settings to make sure that we are aware when anyone takes notice of us. We deeply desire to be seen, known, and quite literally, "liked."

We do this by constantly holding out the empty cups of our lives to be filled by the opinions of others. We run from place to place, activity to activity, person to person, to be filled and loved. And when they like us, we *feel* filled up … for a bit.

What happens when they don't? Or what happens when the good feelings run dry? We feel isolated and empty.

The problem is that we're often holding out empty cups to be filled up by people or things that simply don't have the capacity to fully satisfy our longings or deficiencies. To make things more complicated, other people hold out their empty cups in our directions.

Our lives should not be about trying to fill the emptiness a me-centered life brings. Our lives can be about fixing our focus on God (upward), to be filled (inward), so that we may overflow (outward) in response.

FIXING OUR FOCUS UPWARD

We all know "in the beginning, God created." But this story—*the* Story—began before the beginning. The central character, God, didn't create because He needed something or someone—He was in the glorious community of the Trinity before anything began, a dance of overwhelming life and glory among Father, Son, and Holy Spirit.

He created in order to share the fully loved, fully known, fully accepted life He knew and enjoyed. He created us to be sharers as well.

As we focus upward on Him and His grand redemptive narrative, we, the supporting actors, experience the truest of true life God originally intended before that snake snuck in and convinced humankind otherwise.

The beauty of placing God at the center of our lives is that His love is abounding. Imagine God's love is like Niagara Falls, but even bigger. Imagine you are holding a cup under the waterfall of God's love. With His infinite love and acceptance rushing over in cascades overwhelming our cups, we effortlessly overflow into the lives of others—not from ourselves, but from Him who is at the source, so that He can be their source too.

BEING FILLED INWARD

My (Megan's) husband calls me a "level jumper." Apparently, I have no problem jumping from a conversation about lunch to a "How is your soul?" type of question. He always laughs. I relentlessly remain focused.

Life is too short to ask questions without thinking. We say, "How are you?" as we hustle past because we're too busy to really wait and listen for an honest answer. Most times, I used to answer "Busy" as an excuse to live for myself.

We're all *too* busy. And for me, I had not acknowledged my choice in the matter. This is why I decided to stop using the word "busy." I developed a new go-to answer to the "How are you?" question. "I'm full" became my new response.

"Full" threw people off (apparently they wanted the usual "Good" or "Fine"). I had challenged myself to be honest when they inquired, "Full of what?" In the beginning, most of the time the answer was "Myself." But now occasionally, by God's gracious perspective and changing love, I'm able to say, "Full of God," when I live the truth—that God is central.

FUTILE ATTEMPTS TO FILL OURSELVES

Like the supporting actors throughout Scripture, we still sometimes try to fill ourselves, even though we know we have a better option. Too often we settle for the quick fix of double-tapped social exchanges, but our hearts were created for so much more. This is why the apostle Paul knelt down desperately to pray for the Christians in Ephesus. He prayed to God to fill the inward depths of their lives with Himself:

> I pray that out of his glorious riches he [God] may strengthen you with power through his Spirit in your inner being, so that Christ may dwell in your hearts through faith. And I pray that you, being rooted and established in love, may have power, together with all the Lord's holy people, to grasp how wide and long and high and deep is the love of Christ, and to know this love that surpasses knowledge—that you may be filled to the measure of all the fullness of God. (Eph. 3:16–19)

Paul desperately prayed for the Christians' inner beings. He deeply wanted Christ followers to be filled by God and not rooted in anything or anyone else. We, like the Christians in Ephesus, must depend on God to do for us what we cannot do for ourselves and then tenaciously teach this to the children and students in our ministries.

To do this, we must address our inner beings and acknowledge the ways we've listened to voices other than His. Have you heard them?

- *Make* your family perfect (or at least appear to be perfect) because that's how you'll be respected by others. No one will listen to you if you have an imperfect family.
- *Make* a name for yourself and don't be counted out by revealing your sin to anyone. You're fine. Everyone sins.
- *Have* a good answer to the "What do you do for a living?" question. Then, stand out among your coworkers.
- *Prove* that you deserve to have a higher position or greater influence.
- *Be* perfect. Hide weakness. You're not good enough as you are.
- *Do* something impressive and make sure people notice.
- *Possess* something worth showing off and show it off nonchalantly.

If we put our confidence in and center our lives on *making, having, proving, being, doing,* and *possessing,* and those things shatter, so will we.

Yet, there's good news. Jesus Christ's body was shattered *for you. For me.*

Settle in and take a few deep breaths. Which of the bulleted points resonates with you the most? Look at each one individually. Ask God to reveal how your heart has sought fulfillment in these ways. As uncomfortable as it is, don't move on quickly or breeze past this section. Your inner being (and therefore effectiveness in ministry) is at risk.

As you acknowledge each way you have sought to be filled by someone or something other than God, invite God's immediate presence into that thought. See each thought as an invitation to peel back an inner layer, and open this honest truth about yourself to God in a new way. Thank God for His presence with you during this time of acknowledging.

Rather than being discouraged in large failures, thank Jesus for the ongoing, cup-filling, transforming power of His Spirit to fill you afresh with more of Himself.

OVERFLOW OUTWARD

Having our lives centered on God makes us live for something more than a temporal love that's insatiable. Once we're "filled to the measure of all the fullness of God," we don't need to guard ourselves so jealously. We're moved to love and serve others not out of a need to be loved by them but out of the abundance that is the result of being loved by Him. Our attention becomes less on how the world is affecting us and more on how God can, through us, affect the world.

That's God's game plan. It involves us, but it's not about us. This overflowing kind of life sure beats the overworking that busyness maintains.

THE OPPOSITE OF BUSY

I (Michelle) was greatly impacted by an experience I had in Australia that helped me see the need to slow down and "pause." Culturally, Australians break for tea in the middle of their day. This could include coffee, tea, and savory or sweet treats, but what impacted me even more than what they ate and drank was *how* they paused.

I noted that every time my friend Terry served tea, he did so with china. I noted this because it didn't matter if there were five people or 150 in attendance … we still used china. I commented how special I felt, knowing how much work it is to wash all of those cups. My friend chuckled and said, "Yes, you Americans rush into a coffee shop and get your coffee to go in a paper cup."

I laughed nervously because I was thinking that ducking into a coffee shop and quickly ordering a to-go cup of coffee was normal and even a "treat" for me. I wasn't sure why he was mocking it.

Then he continued, "If you have a paper cup, it suggests that you are on your way somewhere, that you are mobile. If you have a china cup, it suggests that you are present. Pausing. Staying. Being." It wasn't about the tea or the coffee or even the savory treats. It was about taking a moment away from learning, working, running, and thinking to just be present with others.

Imagine our lives if we were to embrace not only this habit but also this way of thinking.

I recently started a new position at my job, and having been influenced by my Australian brothers and sisters, I began "tea at three" every other Wednesday. This was a time for me to gather my entire team of fifteen hardworking individuals and give them a time of pause over tea served in china cups. We don't run away to our cubicles or to a meeting with a snack in hand; rather, we pause for about thirty minutes to catch up on ministry and each other's lives.

I love imagining a new generation of students and families where we slow down together and, in the absence of mind-boggling busyness, we actually come to know God and see Him at work at the *center of our lives* (instead of ancillary to our goals) with greater clarity.

CENTRAL CHARACTER CONFUSION

Eight years into ministering to students, I (Megan) saw God reveal a common thread in the graduated students I had met over the years who were "done with God." The problem wasn't that church services no longer entertained them; it was that the good feelings, peace, and emotional highs they experienced when they worshipped God in middle school or high school had ceased.

Without realizing it, they had made the gospel by-products their gods. When the pursuit of good feelings (and other gospel by-products) became the goal, these students unknowingly placed themselves and their desires at the center of their lives.

God had stopped serving these twentysomethings their spiritual high, so they, in return, quit serving God.

These students (like us) question God's love because it *feels* less palpable than the forty-eight likes they got on their most recent social media pictures. Rather than their lives revolving around God, they merely involve Him in their plans.

God simply becomes one of many influences that might make it to the top of that day's to-do list.

When the children and students we serve place themselves and their desires at the center, they evaluate everyone else on how effectively the others play their supporting roles in the central character's dreamed-up plotline. Their prayers ask God to join their lower-story plans. I say lower, not lesser, because it is through our lives that God initiates His upper, grand plan of redemption for all. Fortunately for us, the real plotline is God's redemption of the world. We can see His plan at work if we, and the students and families we serve, fix our focus on God.

Randy Frazee described our lives as having upper and lower stories. This creates a need for there to be (1) a storyteller and (2) a main character in that story. We don't have a problem recognizing that God is storytelling, but we intuitively think we're the main characters.

Herein lies a problem: students can unknowingly be convinced that they're the central characters. And have you noticed? Parents make great supporting actors. While we absolutely want our parents to support their children, we want them to be supportive of them in the right ways.

If parents support students in their "all about me" lifestyles, everyone and everything, including service opportunities, become ways to further their children's successes. If we're not intentional in how we lead families, they'll become a true product of culture with its blaring ads and blinking lights that smack us in our faces and urge us to "have it our way" or, at least, try to be happier. With cultural influences, the families of today will continue striving for life found *from* God. Primarily concerned with their own satisfaction and pursuit of happiness, students then become more interested in what they can get from God instead of being interested in God Himself. As a result, students develop the belief that God is a mere means to their own personal satisfaction.

How can we cause the families we serve to see God as the end versus the means to their own personal ends? We fix the focus of families onto the upper story line of God—the storyteller *and* central character of their stories.

By the way, we have the best jobs in the world. And remember, our jobs involve power, which is why we must always stay connected to the Source.

This ultimate privilege is about inviting those we serve into the greatest, most epic story line of God redeeming the entire world back to Himself. The plan and purpose are already set in place, and we have an invitation to join *the* story line; it's one you don't want to miss.

We have the opportunity of a lifetime; it's not an obligation. Our roles involve adding more guests to join the upper story by directing their attention upward, creating space for them to personally encounter the living God (inward), that they may live lives of worship in response (outward).

GOD AT THE CENTER OF MINISTRY

Imagine what this could look like. Placing God at the center of ministry would change the goal of every activity, Bible story, discussion, worship expression, personal application, and relationship opportunity. The point of reading the Word would be to reveal God's character so that children, students, and families would truly know Him more and more. Suddenly, the story of David and Goliath, which was never meant to be about David, becomes about God winning a victory.

We can trust that God keeps His covenants because His unchanging character was revealed with Noah. Noah's life becomes less about wood and animals and more about God's presence, covenants, and power.

When we seek God's character in His Word, we begin to awaken curiosity—cultivate a desire to know God more—and begin to take more meaning from God experiences. We become disciplined learners instead of mere reciters. We work to create space for families to become disciples of Jesus who hunger to grow in faith, who are more captivated by the question of *who God is* rather than *what He can do* for us.

WITH JESUS?

Scottie May is a professor at Wheaton College and a prolific author on children's spirituality and faith formation. I (Michelle) admire her immensely. When I first met her, I couldn't even speak because I was so nervous.

I was at the point in my ministry to children, youth, and their families where I was starting to be awakened to some of the things she strongly supported, and she said she'd come visit my ministry. I was a nervous wreck. All day she walked around with a clipboard observing my ministry. I couldn't read her face. At the end she asked me a question that I know she had asked countless people before me. She said, "Michelle, this is so great. I love what you've done. It's fun, it's relevant, it's exciting, and it's excellent. You've done such a great job. But this is my greatest concern: When do the children get to actually *be with* Jesus?"

My heart sank as my defenses rose. Hadn't she seen the kids saying their Bible verses? That was about Jesus. And wasn't she listening during the teaching time, when Jesus was walking on the water? That was about Jesus. And our craft was a picture of Jesus. We even sang songs about Jesus. So what was she talking about?

But her question was deeper than what my rebuttals could offer.

When do your children actually get to *be with* Jesus?

When do they have a chance to pause, be still, and listen to Him?

When can they have a taste of silence from the busy world to talk to Him, speak to Him, and sit with Him in concern or celebration?

Her questions have altered forever the way I minister to children and youth.

We need to make Him central, the focus of all that we do. We need to resist becoming distracted by doing things *about* Him and instead create an environment where children and students encounter Him. How do we create an environment for kids and youth to hear God's voice and just be with Him? What might possibly happen in our midst when we commit ourselves to do that?

GOD STATEMENTS IN LIFE

I (Michelle) had one of my greatest "Aha!" moments about understanding God from reading a book by Robert Mulholland, *Shaped by the Word: The Power of Scripture in Spiritual Formation*. In reading it, I was challenged to view God's Word not as something to merely learn and know but as a conduit for knowing God personally.

Now, this may seem like a "duh" to many, but the forms of teaching and learning that are inherent in the church today suggest to young learners that they are to know "stuff," not necessarily know "God." One of Mulholland's suggestions was to be radically persistent about seeing who God is in any and all passages of Scripture.

This was a fun, new experience for me. So I began: What do I know about God from the narrative of David and Goliath? That was an interesting question, since typically I had learned that David was courageous and trusted God. So to invert the question to be about God and not David was a muscle that hadn't been used as much. I remember sensing the enlightenment as I inwardly shouted, *God is victorious … that's what I know about God from this passage.*

This approach applies to history, poetry, doctrine, and the epistles. Each time I create a God statement for any portion of Scripture, I have a better understanding of the Person with whom I am in relationship. A God statement is a brief, true statement about the character of God that is unchanging or independent of my actions.

Using God statements has transformed the way we both (Michelle and Megan) do community. We talk in God statements, we pray in God statements, and we start team meetings by asking, "What is this week's God statement?" What we're asking is, "How has God revealed Himself to you through the circumstances of the past week of your life?" In the same way we can seek to discover God's character from Moses and David, we can discover more of who God is through our stories as well.

Pausing to see how God has revealed Himself during the week has since become a powerful tradition in the weekly rhythm of our families. We've unified our focus and revealed a new way of worshipping God and loving each other by encouraging, or giving courage to each other by sharing how we see Christ in each other. As a result, we gain courage in Christ.

Intentional conversations with students *can* happen, but they can't be forced—they happen along the way. Seek to initiate a God-centered environment in the home by encouraging (giving courage to) young people with how you see Christ on display through their actions. We're one question away from making God-centered family dinners, car drives, birthdays, and other times together with God-centered questions and traditions.

WHAT IS GOD'S WILL FOR MY LIFE?

One of the most frequently asked questions I (Megan) have received over the years from students is "What is God's will for my life?" I always find this question interesting because it points out what our messages primarily focus on—how this Bible story affects *my* life.

Rather than seeking out God, students primarily focus on how what they heard relates to them. They don't really know how to discern what God might be leading them to do—they've gotten used to a set of instructions catered specifically to how they ought to live for Christ. Of course, giving three-point applications at the conclusion of a message is not wrong, but by prescribing the next step, leaders sometimes remove the opportunity for students to walk in step with God's Spirit.

As ministry leaders, we need to cultivate silence for the people we serve, because silence brings to the surface what is really going on.

For one student, silence may bring out the pain and the questions he has about his parents' divorce. For another, it may come out as the experience of God's love that she hasn't felt in years.

The key to helping them bring their true lives and desires before the living God, with hope of transformation, is to make space for students to meet with the living God and then respond to Him.

Those we minister to don't always need more good advice; they need to develop rhythms in their lives of listening and responding to the central Character's voice.

And listening is not waiting for our turn to talk.

We have an opportunity, through creating quiet space after a message, for kids and students to cultivate a desire to hear God's voice for themselves. This space is essential for students to learn to discern, listen, and then follow the Good Shepherd's leading for a lifetime of faith.

We can discover God's will for our lives by remembering His will for the world and then coming alongside what He is already up to. It's about asking God who He is, where He is moving, and then how He might be leading us to respond. Silence allows that space because it lets us *really* listen, with God "in view."

LIVING "IN VIEW"

We were created out of love to be loved and to love *in response*. But love involves sacrifice. It involves giving of yourself. It's the example of Christ. God paid the price for each of us and made a way for us to be with Him forever. In response, we give Jesus our lives and choose to follow His lead.

In Romans 12, Paul invites us into this sacrificial way of living. We must notice, though, that chapter 12 starts by stating that we live "in *view* of God's mercy," which has been on display throughout chapters 1–11:

- Chapter 1: There is a God who is meant to be central—creation is meant to showcase Creator. But people (that includes us, by the way) began to worship and serve creation instead of Creator.
- Chapter 2: No amount of being good will fix that, because ...
- Chapter 3: We all have a sin issue.
- Chapter 4: It's impossible to fix ourselves.
- Chapter 5: "But God" sent His Son to die. We now have a choice: we can choose to lay down our lives and put God and His sacrifice at the center or continue trying to earn through our efforts.
- Chapter 6: He died because the consequences of sin are grave. *Literally.*
- Chapters 7 and 8: We will still wrestle with our old habits and ways.
- Chapters 8 and 9: But then God reminds us to believe and then surrender. It's a habit we must take on. We fix our focus, believe, and surrender because of the incredible, life-giving example of Christ.

- Chapters 10 and 11: If we confess, "Jesus is Lord"
  and believe in His resurrection, we will be saved.

"Therefore ..." (chapter 12), because He gave His life, we are called to give ours. We're not called to lives of sacrifice in order to gain God's mercy and love; instead, we're called to live in response to God's mercy and love.

I'M TRYING

Our lives are not to be about trying to live well behaved; they are about living "in view" of the Person who offers His perfect, stainless life and living lives of worship in response to that gift.

What does this life of worship look like? It looks like Christ. Worship is not just a spiritual thing; it's an embodied lifestyle. This is one more reason why our daily focus matters.

There is a vast difference between reading the Bible for inspiration and reading the Bible to find the source of all inspiration. When we begin reading God's Word to find God Himself, we have Someone to respond to. The central point of God's Word to us is good news about who God is and what He has done; it is not a list of to-dos.

I (Megan) have asked hundreds of students over the years if they were followers of Jesus. I thought it was an easy yes-or-no question until I noticed multiple students responded with, "Well ... I'm trying." With WWJD bracelets on their wrists, for years I have watched students view Christianity as a life about what they *must* do.

They've missed the central point. They've focused on how they ought to respond rather than truly and intimately knowing God.

We must, therefore, minister first by fixing their focus back to the central point of God's Word—the transforming good news about *What Jesus Has Done!* (WJHD).

I should invest in new bracelets.

RECIPE FOR TRANSFORMATION

Beyond information about Him and inspiration toward Him, you and I need the image of the invisible God, the Firstborn over all creation (Col. 1:15). We need God—the uncreated One. That is something I (Megan) can't even fathom. And maybe that's the point. God is both beyond fathomable and utterly close. How do we respond? Time spent with that question and His presence is a recipe for transformation as He shares out of abundance what we need.

This could move you if you decide not to skip over it. Choose to pause and think about the God who is both beyond fathomable and utterly close.

PRAYER FIXES OUR FOCUS

The best sermons I (Megan) have heard are the ones where I'm left with thoughts of God. Who God is affects how I live, how I discern His voice, and how I respond in life. When our eyes are fixed on Him and our cups are pointed upward, God, the inexhaustible Source of life, love, satisfaction, and peace, uses our stories to further His. And that's the point! Prayer fixes our focus. Let's bring our fears, worries, anxieties, joys, and celebrations before our true King.

Father God, reorient my life to revolve around You. Fix my focus to place You at the center of my life so I may love others in response … not out of need, but out of abundance. Thank You that my life doesn't have to be about sitting and waiting for people to love me, because I'm already fully loved. Amen!

MINISTRY ASSESSMENT

Listen

How do you sense God moving you today? How can you cause the families you serve to fix their focus on Jesus as the end versus the means to their own personal ends? Where might God be calling you to create space for the children or students you serve to spend time with Him?

So What?

God is both the storyteller and central character of *the* Story. If we don't establish a God-centered ministry environment, the families we lead can unknowingly be convinced that they're the central characters. What part might God be asking you to play in the process of making Him central in the lives of the families you serve? How might you inspire families to know and respond to this revelation? What is one next step you can take?

Now What?

As you meditate on who God is, what are the words that come to your mind today? Finish this sentence: "God is …" How has His character shaped you in this past season of life? What is your response to that intervention? How has God revealed Himself to you, and why do you think He has revealed Himself to you in this way?

8

ESSENTIAL SEVEN: A COMMUNITY OF MINISTRY SUPPORT

Equipped for Ministry To, With, and Through

*Coming together is a beginning; keeping together
is progress; working together is success.*[1]

Edward Everett Hale

I wonder if the way you travel reflects how you live. If traveling is as much about the journey as it is the destination, then *how* I'm moving, and with whom I'm choosing to move, matter.

I (Megan) thought I was fully prepared for my two o'clock flight—ride to the airport arranged, carry-on under the size limit. Then I double-checked my flight time at the last minute to discover it was not at two o'clock as I'd planned, but at one o'clock. By the time I arrived at the airport, I had fifteen minutes to get from the curb to the airplane before the doors closed. It wouldn't have been a problem, except for the inevitable two hundred hindrances (or people) in line at security.

Well, here goes nothing, I thought. "Attention, everyone!"

I had the attention of everyone in the security line—rather quickly and not surprisingly.

"Here's the deal," I said. "I thought my flight was at two o'clock, but it turns out it's at one o'clock! And I have ten minutes to get to my gate." Among a crowd full of I'm-embarrassed-for-you facial expressions, I continued with greater passion—"It can be a *community* effort!" I thrust up my pointer finger as I stood in a victory stance. *"Who's with me?"*

No one said anything.

Until …

A five-year-old girl pushed her way to me and matched my pose. "I'm with ya!"

With that, the dam broke and the people parted for me. In three minutes I had made my way to the front of security and turned back in amazement to notice the crowd of strangers cheering me on. I shouted thank you to my new friends as I began to run, *Home Alone* style, through the airport. I saw the airline employees closing the doors as I neared my gate. I shifted gears and sprinted. With grace and chuckles from the flight crew, I was able to board the plane.

That day I did something I rarely do—besides shouting at a crowd of strangers in front of TSA (although that was a first). *I asked for help.*

A family ministry leader friend of mine, Alex Douglas, often asks this question: "Are you a part of the 'I can do it all by myself' club?"

If we focus on the tasks in front of us without looking to the people at our sides, we miss out on the opportunities for ministry closest to us. Getting ministry tasks done alone works for the *tasks*, but it is ineffective for *discipleship*, which, ironically, is the aim of most ministry tasks, isn't it?

Why did you sign up for ministry in the first place? Was it to pull off events? To see a large number of people attend them? Your interest in ministry probably wasn't the numbers themselves but the faces they represented. If you're like me, you signed up to be a part of God's epic story line, part of the greatest story ever told, and to participate in the telling of it.

GOD'S TYPE OF GOOD

Life in the beginning was good. God created the heavens and the earth—good. God created the animals—good. But God created man and woman—*very good*. And by "very good," I can assume humankind was created whole, complete, and lacking nothing we needed to honor and glorify God with our lives. Humankind was created very good in a garden full of good. There was only one thing God said was not good in Genesis 2:18: "It is not good for the man to be alone."

Adam was by himself—"not good." Hear the word of our Lord. It was not good for the man to be alone.

Are you isolated and all alone in ministry?

It's not good.

It's not just a little not good; it's important.

How important do you think community is to God? God—Father, Son, and Holy Spirit, the One who is Himself a community—created us in His image. We were created in the depths of our beings to live in community. Community life is the "good life," the life that speaks to those depths, but sin corrupts what was intended for good. Sin, the invader, whispers to us to find confidence by comparison rather than community through collaboration. Rather than sharing life and work with those around us, we settle for nights alone in front of an iPad (something we can predict and bend to our will).

In C. S. Lewis's *The Great Divorce*,[2] everyone in hell has big houses. Their houses are so big, and so far apart, that damned people never have to see anyone else. They quibble and move away, until they move so far it will take years before they will find another person. They can stay wrapped in the infinitely small hellfire of themselves.

A similar isolation defines our modern Western culture and is the opposite of God's good plan for us.

THE WORK IS TOO HEAVY

I (Megan) had been doing student ministry for ten years when I called Michelle. We had been working together for several years by this time, building a family ministry model that would impact today's generations. I was sacrificing myself to make this happen because I was passionate that it could happen. But, now, I was tired. I was tired beyond comfort or advice but knew a phone call to a trusted friend was necessary. Even though many people surrounded me, Michelle was the one who discerned my burnout and isolation.

In that moment, she didn't give me advice—she just asked me to turn to Exodus 18:13. In the midst of my heavy burden, she knew God's Word would not only expose my heart but also seep deep into my brokenness in ways only God could.

I assumed she would read. She asked if I would.

Thanks, Michelle.

I began to read aloud:

> The next day Moses took his seat to serve as judge
> for the people, and they stood around him from
> morning till evening. When his father-in-law saw
> all that Moses was doing for the people, he said,
> "What is this you are doing for the people? Why do
> you alone sit as judge, while all these people stand
> around you from morning till evening?"
>
> Moses answered him, "Because the people come
> to me to seek God's will. Whenever they have a dispute,
> it is brought to me, and I decide between the parties
> and inform them of God's decrees and instructions."
>
> Moses' father-in-law replied, "What you are doing
> is not good. You and these people who come to you
> will only wear yourselves out. The work is too heavy
> for you; you cannot handle it alone. (Exod. 18:13–18)

I began to cry. What I was doing was not good. I was wearing
myself out. The work was too heavy. Ministry had become too much
for me to handle, and I wasn't meant to carry the load all alone. I
continued reading:

> Listen now to me and I will give you some advice,
> and may God be with you. You must be the people's
> representative before God and bring their disputes
> to him. Teach them his decrees and instructions,

and show them the way they are to live and how they are to behave. But select capable men from all the people—men who fear God, trustworthy men who hate dishonest gain—and appoint them as officials over thousands, hundreds, fifties and tens. Have them serve as judges for the people at all times, but have them bring every difficult case to you; the simple cases they can decide themselves. That will make your load lighter, because they will share it with you. If you do this and God so commands, you will be able to stand the strain, and all these people will go home satisfied. (Exod. 18:19–23)

We have all probably spent too many years in ministry slugging it out by ourselves, on the verge of either burnout or discouragement. Moses was reminded by his father-in-law that there was no reason why Moses should do his ministry work on his own and that things would actually be much better for everyone if the responsibility was shared.

Sharing is necessary, and as the saying goes, "sharing is caring"— but it's also messy and frustrating, and some of the time-sharing work is even slower than doing it alone. But it's absolutely worth it. We can't be fully whole, the way we were meant to be, without a community of ministry support.

INSPIRE, EQUIP, AND SUPPORT

Many Old Testament leaders chose their team members to fulfill *specific* goals. These goals were either commissioned by God or discerned by the leaders. A leader articulated the goal clearly and with detail to those who would help fulfill it—the community of ministry support.

Moses chose faithful men to help judge the Israelites in the wilderness. David and his unmatched mighty men of war conquered some of the vilest armies ever. And Nehemiah and his diverse and talented team rebuilt the wall around Jerusalem against all odds.

Jesus Himself shows us a staff selection process like none other in history. All of history hinged on His choices, and He was intentional about who He chose to be a part of His team. Nowhere in Scripture does Jesus post an ad asking for applications. On the contrary, He was clear about who He wanted, and He sought out each one with an individual invitation.

Although all were invited to follow Him and be changed by God, only twelve men were invited to be part of Jesus's inner circle and His plan to evangelize the entire world. He was tenacious in teaching them to ensure that they were clear on why He was there and what His mission was.

Not only did He understand His disciples' complexities, He seems to have chosen them with diversity in mind. He even chose a disciple He knew would betray Him.

Although sympathetic to their faults and weaknesses, Jesus never allowed His disciples to use these as excuses to become stagnant. His faithful example was indelible on their hearts and minds, and when He returned to heaven, He sent His Holy Spirit to abide with and in them to ensure the mission would continue.

In both Old and New Testament examples, we see three aspects for establishing, developing, and sustaining a community of ministry support:

- *Inspiring* a team toward the goal
- *Equipping* the team precisely for that goal
- *Supporting* the team and situation for the long haul

To *inspire* means we will not barge into our mentor and leadership relationships with huge to-do lists, but rather we will take time to inspire people toward an envisioned future, allowing them to be captured by the path of the mission.

In addition, we can *equip* those in our care. We need to consider what kind of training will allow them to be productive and successful in their positions. If they don't succeed, we must assume part of the responsibility if we have not equipped them with all the necessary resources we have at our disposal.

Support can often be one of the weak areas in our ministries. Where do other staff and volunteers go in grief, sin, mourning, or crisis, or simply when having a bad day? Where do they go to rejoice, celebrate, get motivated, or share audacious ideas?

It should be to their leaders, shouldn't it?

As we begin to *inspire* leaders toward a unified vision, *equip* them for their roles, and establish rhythms of *supporting* them along the way, we're ready to do the work of family ministry.

This is the ministry Psalm 78 commissions us to do: to pass on faith from generation to generation, even to those *yet to be born* (v. 6). Faith that lasts will take more than just me or you or our local church staffs and volunteer leaders. We're going to have to join together for the long haul and not give up.

Sharing ministry with our communities of leaders is among the greatest challenges and blessings in our endeavors of passing on faith to the next generation. In selecting leaders for such a time as this, we must choose individuals with enduring character qualities and gifts who will contribute wholeheartedly to God's family ministry movement. We must have eyes to see beyond the here and now, beyond who gets the "credit," in order to build communities of leaders who understand the mission to change this generation for the sake of Christ and who will be dedicated to this generation's success.

THE ART OF REPLICATION

Leader deficit is a huge issue in ministries. Over the years, ministry leaders have used tactics to attract volunteers because of overwhelming need. Looking back on my (Michelle's) recruiting experiences, no matter how creative my methods were, they simply were never enough.

I remember feelings of discouragement every weekend, when a small group leader was a no-show or we had to close a classroom because of a lack of volunteers. I desperately wanted to work with dedicated people who were serving out of a calling instead of guilt.

About five years ago, I was serving as the family ministry director leading a team of about ten. One week, after our annual "recruitment Sunday, all-church" announcement, I saw my staff members' disappointment with the number of response cards we received. I could tell that they were beginning to lose hope and, worse, lose faith in our mission to children, students, and their families.

Then I had an idea. What if we changed our approach? What if instead of merely trying to recruit and train more volunteers by ourselves, we chose to intentionally invest our time in the replication of the leaders we already had?

At the core, this is the idea of mentorship or discipleship.

In *recruiting*, the person on staff is central (like the axis on a wheel) and all energy or success comes from the abilities of that person.

In *replication*, the person on staff serves as a catalyst to awaken another like-minded individual, who in turn will also reproduce himself or herself in another after a period of time.

While the mathematics of recruiting is *addition*, the mathematics of replication is *multiplication*.

With this idea ignited in my mind, I invited my staff to attend a dinner celebration at my home—one year from the time I extended the invitation. The "ticket" to the celebration was bringing another person—someone whom each person on the team had mentored and discipled in the ways of being a ministry leader. In essence, each person was challenged to make a replica of himself or herself who would join them in ministry.

Once the invitation was made, not much was discussed about it, but it was there on our calendars, staring at us. With a challenge ahead of my staff and a year to complete it, my team set out to accomplish the task, each with a different approach.

A year later, my team of ten had almost doubled in size (not everyone accomplished the goal, which meant not every staff member was allowed to attend the dinner—much to their disappointment).

We spent time eating, celebrating, and storytelling and then ended the night with my staff members affirming their volunteers for the way they had seen dedication and growth in them over the past twelve months.

It was a powerful night. We looked around and realized we were not alone. Not only had each person replicated himself or herself in another, some of those who had been invested in had *already* begun the process as well, and their disciples were with us too. We called these people our "grandkids."

Next, we gave the commission for each person at the table to find another person and do the same process again. Little did we know that within just eighteen months, our senior leadership would decide to expand to a multi-campus model staffed with volunteers rather than paid staff. While many departments found themselves desperate to find leadership, God had gone before us to provide a "deep bench" of passionate individuals to lead each of our campuses.

We realized that recruitment will always be necessary, but instead of merely filling a spot for the sake of getting by, we will now have a small army of community support that stands alongside us in awakening families.

TO, WITH, AND THROUGH

I (Megan) recognized this truth afresh when I stepped off the stage after facilitating one of David C Cook's Family Ministry Conversations. A kind Australian gentleman asked me an interesting question: "Do you think we're meant to do ministry *to* families, *with* families, or *through* families?"

It was a great question. At first I wondered if this man already had a well-thought-out answer to this well-thought-out question, but he didn't—and, at the time, neither did I.

Later, I thought back and tried to remember why I first got involved in vocational ministry: Did I want to minister *to* others, *with* others, or did I envision the potential of ministering *through* others? Could I see a future for those I served that moved past their dependence on me as a leader?

Can you remember why you first got into ministry? Have those reasons or goals changed?

I imagine you first entered ministry with a deep desire to *do ministry* by ministering *to* children or students as you would teach them, mentor them, disciple them, and have fun with them. But at some point you recognized you weren't doing this alone—that you couldn't do it alone. As you moved up the leadership ladder, you may have realized the potential for greater influence as you ministered *to* your fellow leaders.

And then came the ultimate awakening and perhaps the reason you picked up this book. You realized that the biggest influences on the children and students are their families, so you added them to your ministry.

Your fellow leaders and parents need a safe space to be ministered *to* as well, and we can't forget this. Because they've already assumed leadership roles, we sometimes rush them into leader meetings or parent trainings, assuming they're fine—they don't need to be ministered *to*—as we merely equip them with the ministry *how-tos*. But leaders and parents are just as broken as anyone else. As they experience transformational grace, they're more likely to spill over and model authentic vulnerability and transformation to those they lead.

PULLING AN "ADAM AND EVE"

When I (Megan) was a student, I wondered if the point of attending youth ministry was to bring my sin out in the open and expect God to minister *to* me on a weekly basis. I trusted Jesus to meet my sin with forgiveness, but being ministered *to* weekly at youth group felt like an awfully vicious pattern: come drenched in sin and ugliness, humbly and courageously confess my sins to God and others, and then find restoration with the cross in focus yet again.

And again.

And then look forward to the same pattern the following week.

It seemed much more enticing to pull an "Adam and Eve" and hide. I found it was a lot easier to choose homework instead of youth group half the time, because being ministered *to* is as tiring for the recipient as it is for the minister, and I didn't want to be a burden.

Is ministering *to* people the goal? Is that church? Is that what our families have experienced? Do they have a vision beyond a churchy car wash, bringing their mess to be temporarily cleaned up until next week? There had to be more.

Guess what? There is.

As you expand your responsibilities and minister *to* children or students, leaders, and parents, you can expand your reach vastly as you ask another question: *Why do we minister to these groups of people?*

JOINING THE MISSION OF REDEMPTION

We minister *to* them so we can minister *with* them. As you pour into the lives of your children or students, leaders, and parents, if you let them, they can begin to join you in the work of the ministry. You bring them in on it. As we approach God's throne of grace with confidence, He ministers *to* us in our times of need (Heb. 4:12–14), and as He does, He equips us with His presence to do the work of ministry *with* Him.

Our ministries can work the same way God does—we are not only ministered *to* by His Spirit, but we are also called to minister *with* God—just as in Ephesians 4:11–13 when Paul charged all Christians with this job description:

> So Christ himself gave the apostles, the prophets, the evangelists, the pastors and teachers, *to equip his people for works of service,* so that the body of Christ may be built up until we all reach unity in the faith and in the knowledge of the Son of God and become mature, attaining to the whole measure of the fullness of Christ.

For years, I've heard leaders complain about families being passive recipients in church; now I see a clear next step. Leaders can provide opportunities for those "not standing on a stage vocationally" to minister *with* them so they don't fall into the malaise of church consumerism, simply coming to get a spiritual high and then leaving it in the building. Leaders need to share the ministries. As they do, they'll be in awe and wonder of God's movements within those ministries.

My friend Jeff Bachman is one of the most passionate student ministry leaders I know. Not only is he passionate, he is also generous; he shares his ministry *with* his students. Hear from one of his students, Mea, who experienced the joy of ministry after Jeff prepared and equipped her to share a message with her peers:

> It was really uplifting for me! Part of what I spoke about was something I was always afraid to share with people. After speaking, it took this crazy weight off my back and I felt so much more at peace and loved. I taught that God wants us to live in biblical community. God taught me to trust in Him and in my community. Now, I'm a lot more open with people because you never know, they could be going through the same thing or it might even give them a sense of hope or encourage them to be open and honest as well! There's no holding back or hiding for me anymore.

Students need opportunities to minister *with* leaders in a safe environment where they can honestly and vulnerably share their faith. As they do, we'll come to watch them own their faith. Without it, our ministries may end up as just another service they consume, like Spotify or Netflix. Students fall back into a consumerist posture when they don't know any other way, so they remain stagnate.

KIDS MINISTERING *TO* KIDS *WITH* US

Several years ago I (Michelle) was leading a group of elementary students through the book of James. At the conclusion of our eight-week study, I was compelled by this idea of wanting them to flex their faith muscles. I didn't plan a new study right away. I wanted to take our next time together to explore what could follow. The kids arrived and sat down as usual to hear the next Bible study, but this time there wasn't one.

Instead I asked them, "Children, how can *you* put your faith into action? You've heard these things from God's Word for the past eight weeks. You've learned that God wants us to not just be 'hearers' of His Word but 'doers' also. So, what are you going to *do* about what you've *heard*?"

At first there was silence. The kids just stared back at me. I realized that I had never asked them such a thing. This wasn't what they were expecting. They didn't know how to answer. So I kept pressing, asking them to ask God how they might respond to what they had heard.

I confess there was a part of me that desperately wanted to validate my teaching and give them suggestions for action steps they could simply agree with. I didn't want to consider that with all we had done to truly investigate Scripture, it had fallen into the abyss of biblical information stored securely away in the archives of a child's brain. No! I wanted to see *life transformation*. If I'm honest, I wanted to know that God was still in the business of raising up individuals whose faith "the world was not worthy of" (Heb. 11:38).

I didn't give in to my desire to push them in the right direction. At this point, my faith was hanging in the balance as much as theirs was. "What are you going to do now that you have heard the words of God and how He wants us to live?" It felt like an eternity in waiting. I was uncomfortable. My leaders were uncomfortable. The kids were … well, bored.

But then one courageous hand rose in the back. The young girl said, "We could help the homeless people."

My heart leaped. "Yes, we could do that! What else could we do to put our faith into action?" I asked. Soon more children began to chime in with ideas that ranged from eliminating global hunger to knitting sweaters for cold dogs.

AN IDEA FLESHED OUT

After some hearty brainstorming, we finally landed on an idea that was actually doable. Our church was in relationship with a local motel ministry. Families who had been displaced from their homes or were in some kind of transition, including fleeing from abuse, lived there. The idea of packing sack lunches for those families so that the children would have healthy meals at school ignited excitement in our group. We were about to do ministry *with* and *through* the kids in our church!

In order for them to further flex their faith muscles, we asked the kids to come up with how we would mobilize this, how we would gather the lunch supplies, and even what items would go into the lunches. Of course it would have been easier to give the idea to a group of moms and have them work out the details, but the kids were the ones who were supposed to be learning to discern God's voice.

I was encouraged to see that with a little guidance, they all worked together and made great decisions about what should go into the lunch bags. Then one child said, "We can't forget the note." Ah, the note. This one child stated that his favorite part of lunch at school was the note from his mom. So we started talking about how this note could be a note *from God*.

The day finally arrived for us to assemble the lunches. Stations were set up all over the room to decorate the lunch bags, make the sandwiches, and fill the bags with chips or pieces of fruit. There was one station where the kids could write the "notes from God." I printed out note cards that said "Dear one" on the top, had a blank area (for the child to write a note), and then closed with "Love, God."

At first I felt the need to help them. After all, writing on behalf of God was serious business. I didn't want them to get it wrong. I took out a whiteboard and began to write suggested things God might say to a person in such a situation.

No sooner had my hand begun to write on the whiteboard than I felt convicted. God's Spirit was urging me, "Don't you believe that I can speak to these children? Don't you want Me to be the One who works through them? Don't you want these children to use faith to listen to Me?"

I realized this was how this whole thing began in the first place. I had a desire for these kids to flex their faith muscles, and yet here I was offering to lift the "weight" for them.

I quickly erased my trite words from the board and encouraged the children to pray and ask *God* what they should write. I began to tell them that *God* knew who was going to get their notes. I told them there was something *He* wanted to say to each child who would receive a lunch and He could use their faith to accomplish this. I watched those kids pray as I had never seen them pray before.

One girl, I noticed, would pray, then write, then pray again, then write some more. It was as if she were penning actual words from God. We packed over four hundred lunches that night, and we tucked a little note in each one. In faith, we waited.

A LOVE NOTE FROM GOD

The next day, our representative to the motel went from door to door, passing out a lunch bag to each child. He came to a room where a mom cautiously opened the door and peeked out. She accepted the two lunches for her children, then humbly asked if she could take one for herself. He handed her another lunch and closed the door.

What nobody knew was that early that morning, this mom had woken up in total desperation. She had just been through an ugly divorce. She had been physically abused; she had lost her home and her job. She had nothing. She was now living in this motel with her two kids, and life had lost all hope.

As the reality of the day set in, she began to cry out to God, lamenting, "You've forgotten me, *You've forgotten me!*" In this moment of hopelessness, she decided to end her life. She had arranged for her children to go to school and be picked up by her sister, and while her children were gone, she would kill herself in order to stop the suffering.

As her two children left for school as planned, she saw her lunch bag sitting on the counter. One of the children had decorated the outside of the bag with a beautiful cross beside a colorful rainbow. This woman remembered being a little girl who went to church and heard about Jesus, but she had long since felt forgotten, used, and abused.

Yet something in her reached out and grabbed that lunch. As she looked inside, the very first thing she pulled out was the little note. With trembling hands, she opened it to read these words: "Dear one, I have *not forgotten you*. Love, God."

FAITH INEXTINGUISHABLE

It's almost unbelievable, isn't it? God spoke to a child to write those words. Then God made sure *that note* got placed in *that lunch* for *that mom* on *that day*. Who is this God we serve? He is a God who never forgets and always redeems! His story is one of redemption, and we have the opportunity to play a part in it.

The faith stories of the kids in our ministries are not ones of us simply telling them *what* to do; rather, they are stories of giving them the *opportunity to do it with us.*

The testimony of this woman's life and her experience that day revolutionized the kids' faith when they heard about it. They were radically changed. Their faith had been tested and put into action, and now they would never see their mission in life the same.

Quite simply, they were unstoppable. Before their years of middle school were completed, they had started more ministry opportunities in our community than could be counted. They walked dogs for the elderly, knitted blankets for the homeless in the inner city, bought Bibles for schoolmates, sent care packages to those in the armed services, and sang to shut-ins in retirement homes, just to name a few. And I believe that the world was not worthy of them.

LIVE BY FAITH

Certainly, not every time we ask our kids to enter into ministry with us will something so miraculous happen. Perhaps we will see the fruit, and perhaps we won't. But the God we serve is capable of life transformation. Whether we see it or not is secondary. Our faith comes into play again as we continue to put it into practice regardless of the outcomes our eyes can see. We live it out … by faith.

Parents, too, need opportunities to partner *with* the church. George Barna identified consistencies in the background of mature Christians: "We usually found a symbiotic partnership between their parents and their church." He discovered that "the church encouraged parents to prioritize the spiritual development of their children and worked hard to equip them for that challenge. Parents, for their part, raised their children in the context of a faith-based community that provided security, belonging, spiritual and moral education, and accountability. Neither the parents nor the church could have done it alone."[3]

Parents not only need reminders that they're the primary children's or youth pastors, but they also need entry points within the church ministry. By including parents on ministry trips, asking for them to help create vision statements, inviting them to invest in the lives of the volunteer leaders, and implementing Parent Shepherd leaders (as outlined in chapter 2), parents will move from passive recipients of the church's ministry to co-laborers with the church in God's ministry.

MINISTRY FROM STUDENTS *TO* PARENTS

Lastly, as you minister *with* families, you inspire, equip, and support them to become vessels that God ministers *through*. With God's abundant grace running *through* their lives, we'll get to see the overflow into the lives of their friends, families, and coworkers as they minister beyond the walls of the church.

And the true sign of a disciple is a disciplined learner who is transformed by grace and responds by overflowing that grace outward to the people God has specifically put in their lives.

One of the difficulties in empowering family as primary is, "What do you do about the spiritually orphaned child?" We cannot assume that every parent of our children and students is pursuing a relationship with Jesus.

As we create an environment for children and students to meet and be transformed by the living God, and then give them opportunities to practice ministry, we'll have opportunities *through* them *to* reach their parents. Family is still primary for the passing on of faith! There's nothing more convincing of Christianity than experiencing a spiritually dead person raised to life, especially within your household, especially when the one transformed is a teenager.

In this way, ministry leaders will have not only ministered *to* students and *with* them but also *through* them. An envisioned future of having influence and experiencing life change with loved ones is something people get excited about.

In light of this, we offer this simple way of thinking about your community of ministry support: you minister *to* families and leaders and create environments where you can minister *with* them (all of them) in hopes of ministering *through* them into the places and people you could never reach yourself.

This is something we can see happen — people surrendering their lives to Jesus outside the walls of our churches. It's hardly something we came up with. God never blesses us with vision or transformation merely for ourselves. He doesn't just save us *from* our sins; He saves us *for* a purpose. We are brought out of the fire only to be put into it again. This purpose, this mission, this job, requires power, and we can receive that power as God's ministry bends and tempers us into the likeness of Christ. And by the power of the Holy Spirit's presence, He commissions us to make disciples and redeem the world back to Himself *through* us.

What's more, as you keep these goals in mind, you will end up being ministered to *by* your community of ministry support. This labor of love often comes back to you like a boomerang of blessing.

So, my dear family ministry leader and relationship facilitator, don't minimize your ministry or neglect the opportunities before you. You do so much more than minister *to* children and students; you envision more for them and their families. Realize it, run with it, and rejoice in it.

You're not alone.

MINISTRY ASSESSMENT

Listen

Why did you sign up for ministry in the first place? Who do you consider to be a part of your community of ministry support? How has your role served to inspire them? Equip them? Support them?

So What?

We cannot do ministry alone, and the more we can minister *to*, *with*, and *through* families and leaders, the more we can bring the reign of Christ to this world. Where can you create space for everyone involved in your ministry to be ministered *to*? In what ways can you empower children or students, their parents, and leaders to join *with* you in ministry? Where can you encourage them to be vessels *through* which God reaches their communities of family and friends? How can you create consistent space for them to share stories in order to remember and celebrate their own ministry moments?

Now What?

Take initiative and get involved. You have much to learn and much to gain as we move forward in this family ministry movement together. It may seem like a hard step to find people to be in community with, but we have to do it to keep ourselves and those we minister *to*, *with*, and *through* healthy, and it's not as hard as it may sound. Many curriculum companies and ministry organizations offer community within their resources. Take a bold step, reach out, and find out how to get connected with these resources via social media, conferences, or being a part of a preconference event. Consider this book an invitation to join us at David C Cook's The Gathering—an annual event for family ministry and spiritual formation, a beautiful homecoming of the global faith community of family ministry support. To find out more, visit dccgathering.com.

9

GETTING SET TO LEAD A NEW GENERATION

Becoming a Spiritually Healthy Leader

*The authority by which the leader who follows Christ operates,
is not power but love, not force but example, not coercion but
reasoned persuasion. Leaders have power, but power is safe only
in the hands of those who humble themselves to serve.*[1]

John Stott

Now that we've completed our journey through the seven family ministry essentials, we'll go back to where we began. The family ministry movement we're privileged to be a part of is *God's idea*. He initiated it, He started it, He sustains it, and He is the leader of it. The transformational weight of the world is not on our shoulders.

God is building His church, and the gates of hell will not prevail against it (Matt. 16:18). He has invited us to play a part in the building—God, who could do everything by Himself better than we can do it with Him, graciously invites us to help lead a new generation into the path of the Divine, to create essential family ministry environments that give the Holy Spirit space to move. If we want to partake with God in this glorious mission to a young generation, our foremost move should not be leadership but "followership." You can learn a lot about a leader by looking at whom he or she follows.

FOLLOWING THE LEADER

Remember the game we played as children, follow the leader? Spiritually healthy leadership is less about leading and more about following the Leader. Our Leader. Our Lord and Savior.

Follow the leader was a fun game to play when we were children, giggling through the playground, wondering where the child leader would take us. But as we age, we demand to know where we are going, and we usually want to be the one controlling the destination. Not a lot of giggling is heard when a group of grown adults are competing to take charge.

Sometimes we think that spiritually healthy leadership is about being perfect or dynamic or even clever. But it's actually about allowing God to be in His rightful position of leadership and then helping people follow and depend on the One who is ultimately equipped to lead.

We must follow so that the people entrusted into our care can follow too. Are we dependent on the Holy Spirit to move through our ministry, or have we gotten pretty good at our jobs?

As we learn to depend on God's leading instead of our own skills, we will learn how to lead others to the very Person we all need—the One who restores brokenness and brings dead things to life. It's not always easy. Letting God lead takes discipline to recognize where He's moving and courage to follow Him wherever He goes.

Restoration and healing are impossible tasks if the weight of transformation falls completely on our shoulders, because we weren't meant to work that way. There is no rest for the weary if it's all up to us.

As Timothy Keller put it, "You can do this ministry with God's help—so give it all you've got. You can't do this ministry without God's help—so be at peace."[2] As leaders, we need to trust in God's plan and know that His power can accomplish it.

Spiritually healthy leaders are followers first and leaders second.

The order matters because when talented, innovative, and influential Christian leaders forget that their primary job is to follow Jesus, they've failed. We weren't meant to bear the full load … we *can't* carry all of it. Sometimes the failure to follow Christ looks like a major breakdown, but other times it looks like a leader who is no longer dependent on God to move.

Heed this warning—both are failures.

Dependence on ourselves will breed anxiety and worry, whereas dependence on God will lead us to spiritual health. Our spiritual health is crucial because it spills over into the lives of those we lead.

When Jesus called some of His first followers to join Him in redeeming the world back to Himself in Matthew 4, He initiated. Jesus invited the fishermen to *follow Him* and become part of the miraculous movement He was about to begin.

These fishermen chose to say yes to following Him first and then began leading others second. Following Jesus and fishing for others to experience Him is the call, and this call requires spiritually healthy leaders who know that the movement is much larger than they are.

Spiritually healthy leadership is a call to follow *the* Leader. Jesus didn't ask His followers to lead the first-century churches because of their credentials (backwater fishermen in their twenties didn't have many of those); He called them to lead because He trusted them to follow.

And He brought you in to lead because He trusts you to follow.

LEADERSHIP LIST OF DOS AND DON'TS

What comes to mind when you think of a spiritually healthy leader? Is it someone who spends time in God's Word? Remains morally pure? Someone with a bunch of checkmarks next to things they're abstaining from? I'm sure we could come up with a list of qualities, and I'm sure that list would be cumbersome and exhausting. It makes me wonder, is a spiritually healthy leader based on a definition of actions, or rather is it the posture of one's heart?

In *Becoming a Spiritually Healthy Family*, Michelle used the metaphor of the Director and the Director's chair. She voiced the dilemma a leader faces when he or she attempts to take over the Director's chair. "We grab a pen, write a script, and try to steer the story in the direction we think it should go."[3] In those moments, we have forgotten the entire story, the main Character, and the reason the story was written.

Have you been seated in the Director's chair lately? Are you feeling the weight and responsibility of directing your own life and then the lives of others? If so, take a deep breath. Remember your supporting role, listen to the Director, step down from the chair, focus on the script He has written, and then play the part He assigned for you to play.

Take a quick assessment and ask yourself these questions: In what areas am I attempting to play the role of the Director? Do I fight for influence or control? Do I feel the need to be heard? Am I waiting to be noticed? Do I desire acknowledgment? How about airtime onstage? Have I been enamored with my creativity, excellent programs, engaging speaking style, room decor, or newest innovative message series?

If you said yes to any of those questions, there's hope. God is inviting you to surrender the pen and live abundantly "on script" in the part He's written for you. God, the master storyteller, is up to something great, using spiritually healthy leaders whose lives involve submission and listening to the true Director.

The question then becomes, how might leaders pass on this spiritually healthy lifestyle for others? As we come to know spiritually healthy leadership as "followership," we can model the spiritually healthy life as more than a list of dos and don'ts.

How might God be calling you to lead families as you step down from the Director's chair? How might dependence on His direction change how you teach, how you do leadership training, or how you lead a retreat or outreach event?

How confident are you in discerning God's voice as He leads? Have you heard His voice lately? If so, what has He been saying?

If you haven't listened or heard His voice in a while, do you trust Him enough to wait for it? It will come.

When we surrender our plans and become dependent on God revealing His, we get to see what God's power can do. Rather than hoping for families just to understand and apply, we create opportunities for them to listen, discern, and obey—opportunities to experience God's movement like Bryan Pogue's middle school girls did.

OPPORTUNITIES TO LISTEN, DISCERN, AND OBEY

Bryan Pogue has pastored student ministries for more than ten years. He read Michelle's book *Spiritual Parenting*[4] and came to see that his role as a spiritual parent and leader was not to give application steps but rather to create environments where people could discern God's leading in their own lives. For this reason, he decided to switch up his typical annual "Serve Day" by putting a different leader at the helm—*the Holy Spirit*.

The students were excited to find out Bryan's plan for serving their city as they poured into the student ministry building on a Saturday morning. Someone asked, "So, how and where are we going to serve today?"

"Great question," Bryan responded. "I can't wait to find out!"

To their surprise, Bryan said that this service experience was going to be led by God Himself. The students waited for Bryan to admit he was joking. He told them to get to work. In small groups, the students and their leaders read scriptures together and then drove around their city in silence, listening for how the Holy Spirit would speak and lead them to respond. At first this might sound a bit crazy, but Bryan was forcing the "awkward" in order to bring out something more than passivity among his students.

After their "listening drive," one group of middle school girls discovered that God had highlighted what they called the "older folks' home," one of the hundreds of buildings they drove past. Each girl in the small group had felt a pull to that same building; God was obviously not so silent on their drive.

The girls decided collectively to serve at the convalescent home, and after visiting with the patients for a half hour, they joined in on a dance party for the residents.

And so they danced.

Much to the surprise of the middle school girls, an older gentleman asked about their faith and eventually surrendered his life to Jesus because of their trip. The girls were stunned. They couldn't wait to get back to the church to tell their friends, and eventually their families, about how their surrendered plans, listening for God's leading, and obedience to His call led them to see a spiritually dead man brought to life.

Our responsibility to those we lead is simply to create ministry environments that reveal who God is through His Word, create space for children and students to discern His voice and leading, and encourage them to obey Him by the power of the Holy Spirit.

On this particular not-so-typical "Serve Day," these middle school girls learned firsthand what it means to follow God's leading instead of merely getting an outline of what it *might look like*.

THE SEVEN FAMILY MINISTRY ESSENTIAL ENVIRONMENTS

The seven family ministry essentials are not a list of to-dos—they're environments to create a culture. They align us to come alongside what the Holy Spirit is doing in the lives of those we lead, so they can become spiritually healthy leaders themselves. As most people know, maintaining physical health involves both food *and* exercise. Therefore, it's not enough for families to be *fed* truth; it's essential for them to *exercise* their faith.

Attending church, spending time quietly with God, and reading His Word can feed them effectively, but they need the second part to be truly effective: exercise. It is the role of the family ministry leader to feed families and then create environments for them to exercise their faith.

"THE END"

Leaders need to catch and then engage God's vision for families so those we lead can follow His lead as well. Yet we must first acknowledge that the implementation of the family ministry essentials requires change.

The words *the end* mark for us a poetic conclusion to our favorite stories or movies, to tell us it's over and it's time to leave. But have you ever shouted at the screen as the credits rolled because you didn't want the movie to end? You wanted the story line to continue—you wanted to know what happened next?

At the end of one such movie, I (Michelle) was furious that the director had done this to us. I say "us," but everyone else seemed satisfied with the ending and was leaving the theater. Not me. That was not the end as far as I was concerned—it was only the beginning.

So I sat there in the dark theater, playing out how the plot would go if the end were actually the new beginning. After I had worked it out to my satisfaction, I left my seat, a perfectly thought-out future for the characters planned in my mind.

It's not as clean as that in ministry, but people respond to change in much the same way. Some people see endings as simply that—they pick up their popcorn and move on. Others see endings as tragic and will do anything to prevent the end from occurring, and still others fight to see the ending as only the beginning of something better.

I have been blindsided by how many responses can occur during a process of change, even within a single church or ministry team. In one ministry position in which I had been commissioned to lead change, I was attempting to bring a culture of spiritual parenting where there had been none, and I met every kind of response.

Desiring to see parents live in their rightful roles as the spiritual leaders of their children, I began programs, campaigns, and structures that would let them get more involved in the spiritual lives of their children. Some on my team were passive-aggressive, some were aggressive-aggressive—a few were even passive-depressive. I had those who loved this change as if they had won the lottery, but their joy was squelched by the disapproval of the rest of the group. Anticipating diverse responses will help you manage your expectations of the rate and pace of change.

William Bridges, in his book *Managing Transitions*, suggested four steps in managing the beginning of the change process:

explain the basic *purpose*, paint a *picture*, lay out a *plan*, and give each person a *part* to play.[5] I think of purpose and picture as one element: *vision*.

THE POWER OF VISION

John Kotter reminded leaders in his book *Leading Change* that in trying to bring change, nothing is more important than clarifying and communicating the vision. "*Vision* refers to a picture of the future with some implicit or explicit commentary on why people should strive to create that future," he said.[6] Groups need a vision because it helps align and inspire them into action.

In our ministries, those of us who are responsible for creating vision are ultimately responsible for discerning God's vision. To catch God's vision we need to see that God is always at work around us and that He invites us to become involved with Him in His work, to come alongside what He is already doing. As Christian leaders, we are sometimes tempted to make plans and then ask for God's blessing on them as an afterthought—and then we're surprised when our plans fall flat.

Instead, we need to find God's vision and then make it into something concrete for those we lead. Moses did just this when he shared with the people of Israel the vision God had given him of the Promised Land as a land flowing with milk and honey.

Once people have a picture of the destination, the *plan* to get there becomes crucial. They need detailed steps and schedules that will allow them to have short-term wins and understand exactly what they need to focus on.

GIVE IT AWAY

Lastly, each person needs a *part to play*. Communicating the purpose, picture, and plan is very inspiring, but until each member has a part to play, true transition will not happen at every level. One of the biggest mistakes I ever made as a leader was to "get it done." By this I mean that *I* got it done.

As leaders, we can see the future clearly, and we want to make it happen; so if things don't move as quickly as we'd like, we just do it ourselves. It's much easier in the short term to get it done ourselves. "I'll just do it myself" rings in our ears, and it takes enormous discipline to give each team member a part to play.

No matter how small the role, everyone must take part. Jesus could have stayed on earth and ministered to everyone Himself—He could have brought everyone to Himself by Himself until the whole world was redeemed. But He invited a bunch of peasants to join Him, and He graciously allowed them to be a part of His grand redemptive story. We need to follow Jesus's example.

History, community, camaraderie, and ownership are all by-products of giving away leadership and information. No one ever achieves anything great by doing it alone. Someone might achieve awe, envy, mistrust, and jealousy, but nothing worthy comes from hoarded leadership. *Give it away!*

VOW OF SILENCE

For a few years I (Megan) taught spiritual health and wellness classes at a Christian university. At the start of each week, I would ask if anybody did anything interesting over the weekend. Usually there were one or two stories about trips or birthdays.

"I took a vow of silence," one student said. He explained how he refused to talk over the whole weekend and said, "You should try it...."

I smiled a grin full of mischief and mouthed, "Okay."

At first no one believed it, but after a minute it sunk in. I stared them down. The room crackled with nervous energy. I heard, "No, wait, she can't be serious."

I was. My voice had left the room.

It seems like a teacher needs to talk, but that Monday I learned I could lead just as effectively by giving leadership away.

I went through the whole class without a voice, but instead of awkward stares, a student walked up on eggshells and started to read from my slides, and after a minute he began adding his own commentary. If he didn't know about something, someone else spoke up. The students were more engaged than I had ever seen before. My students became the leaders, and I became a student as I learned the value of a voice, and not just my own. As I watched the students grapple with the topics and take furious notes, I realized the importance of giving away leadership.

SETTING GOALS TOGETHER

A leader of great people will set forth a basic goal or idea and allow the team to pool resources, gifts, and creativity to figure out how to get there. This model takes an effective but humble leader who is willing to allow his or her staff to share in the molding of the vision.

This model, as opposed to that of a more typical executive leader, is far more powerful because every member of the team has a piece of himself or herself in the vision. The plan is in the DNA of the group. On the other hand, the executive leader will seem successful and can even create a dynastic feel during his leadership, but the many worker bees he has enlisted to achieve "his" goal will be left visionless when he leaves.

Great leaders, said Seth Godin in his book *Tribes*, are not concerned with who gets the credit or whether they are getting more opportunities for themselves—they're concerned with the mission of the tribe. They want the mission to succeed and those around them to succeed as well.[7]

Godin highlighted that our world is in desperate need of leaders and that we cannot afford to cower in fear of making mistakes. We will make mistakes. So what? Let's get on with the mission at hand, learning and leading from those very mistakes with greater clarity and confidence.

We cannot afford for our influence to benefit those we serve only while we're with them. We have to find people with enduring character and gifts to take part wholeheartedly in the church's mission after we've left if we are going to change this generation for the sake of Christ. We must look beyond here and now, and beyond who gets the credit, to build lasting teams that, with or without our leadership, understand the mission and will be dedicated to its success.

COMMUNICATING THE GOAL

Once the team has been chosen, inspired, equipped, and supported, keeping the vision clear is essential. Think about your team as it is today. Can they articulate the goal? Is everyone doing a lot of "good stuff," or are they aligning their efforts toward a common vision? A mission?

When we talk about vision, we are referring to the foresight of something that could be. It's important to note a mission differs from vision in that it gives *purpose* to an organization's vision. It tells us *how* we will arrive at the articulated vision and *why* we would consider toiling to do so. It is descriptive in language and should also inspire the hearer. People will not follow a leader without an inspiring vision and a tangible mission plan.

Sometimes it seems that tireless effort achieves a goal, but it doesn't unless it's focused toward that goal. Think of the missions that were set forth in Scripture for a people called to the vision of salvation:

- The mission of leaving one's home to lead a group of people set apart (Abraham)
- The mission of living as holy people in the wilderness, trusting in God alone as their source of provision (Moses with the children of Israel)
- The mission of completely purging Canaan of unholy nations in pursuit of the Promised Land (Joshua and the twelve tribes)
- The mission of rebuilding the city of Jerusalem and its walls (Ezra and Nehemiah)
- The mission of following Jesus and His new covenant (the twelve disciples)
- The mission of proclaiming the gospel in the power of the Holy Spirit until Jesus returns (the Great Commission)

Each of these missions had clear, defining guidelines. Abraham was to leave his land, trust completely in the birth of a son in old age, and wait twenty-five years for the fulfillment. Moses was given the Ten Commandments, among other Jewish laws, to govern the Israelites' time together as a holy community. Joshua was given strict instructions for conquering the land and would prosper only according to the standards given. Ezra and Nehemiah faced opposition but held firm to the focus of a holy city in order to have a place of worship for their people. The disciples were instructed countless times on what it meant to be a disciple.

Those filled with the Spirit of God continue to be instructed throughout the New Testament on what it means to walk in step with Him for the sake of the gospel.

Clarity of mission brings unity and also weeds out those who are just along for the ride. It allows a leader to look each person in the eye and say, "Are you in?" Those who are not will eventually leave, and those who stay will make the mission clearer as they pursue it themselves.

STAYING THE COURSE

Moses, Joshua, Isaiah, Jeremiah, Nehemiah, Jesus, Peter, and Paul committed themselves to the long haul of ministry with those entrusted to their care. They all had chances to get fed up and walk away. They probably did get fed up. But each of these men recognized God's specific call on their lives, and they knew only God could release them from leadership.

As Christian leaders mobilizing diverse staffs in the twenty-first century, we have been commissioned to lead as long as God calls us to. The people who have had the deepest impact on our lives aren't always the ones who wowed us with their talent or insights, but the ones whom we've simply done life with. They have encouraged and comforted us through the difficult times and cheered us on from the sidelines during our snatches of fame. They see us for who we are, and they accept both the most radiating qualities of our Father in us and the things we hoped no one would discover. These people love us anyway.

At the end of the day or year or season, a new generation will be swayed most by the presence of abundant love. There are many staff development models in the world of management, but the model that most reflects Christ, the model that most draws others to become like Him, is the model of love.

This is the same love that hung bleeding on the cross and the same love that breathes life into broken lives today, the love that will transform the world if we let it. We can't afford *not* to love, and we can't afford for our staff members *not* to be transformed by it. For if we can really take part in God's grand story to redeem the world, and if we want to minister *to*, *with*, and *through* families as part of that story, we need to follow that Love who loved the world into being, to be open to His leading, and to let this Love flow through us to a new generation of families in our world.

MINISTRY ASSESSMENT

Listen

Think back on your season of ministry. How have you led? In a team? In isolation? What emotions surround each of those words? What factors contributed to your leading in those ways? What changes do you desire to make? In what areas can you grow? In what areas can you celebrate?

So What?

God is on the move through family ministry. Which family ministry essential is strong in your ministry? Which is not so strong? What is God saying to you about the essentials? In what ways has God awakened you to a potential blind spot in your current ministry? Ask God how He might be leading you to design a ministry based on the family ministry essentials, but specifically crafted for your church and your people and with God's plans for you in mind.

Now What?

It's essential that we play our part and follow the Leader as we lead a new generation to do the same. As you finish this book, what is one practical step you can take to begin implementing each of the seven family ministry essentials?

1. Empowering Family as Primary
2. Spiritual Formation for Lifetime Faith

3. Scripture Is Our Authority

4. The Holy Spirit Teaches

5. God's Grand Redemptive Narrative

6. God Is Central

7. A Community of Ministry Support

NOTES

CHAPTER 1: WHAT IF WE WERE INVITED INTO SOMETHING BIG?

1. Les Brown, *Power to Change* (Chicago: TeleVideo, n.d.), DVD.

CHAPTER 2: ESSENTIAL ONE: EMPOWERING FAMILY AS PRIMARY

1. Holly Catterton Allen, ed., *Nurturing Children's Spirituality: Christian Perspectives and Best Practices* (Eugene, OR: Cascade Books, 2008), 242.

2. George Barna, *Transforming Children into Spiritual Champions: Why Children Should Be Your Church's #1 Priority* (Ventura, CA: Regal, 2003), 28.

3. Mark DeVries, *Family-Based Youth Ministry*, 2nd ed. (Downers Grove, IL: InterVarsity, 2004), 102.

4. The following ten environments material is adapted from Michelle Anthony's book *Spiritual Parenting: An Awakening for Today's Families* (Colorado Springs: David C Cook, 2010).

CHAPTER 3: ESSENTIAL TWO: SPIRITUAL FORMATION FOR LIFETIME FAITH

1. Ruth Haley Barton, *Strengthening the Soul of Your Leadership: Seeking God in the Crucible of Ministry* (Downers Grove, IL: InterVarsity, 2008), 16.

2. Three temptations material developed from Kit Rae, personal conversation with Michelle Anthony, used with permission.

3. Barrett Johnson, "How to Raise a Pagan Kid in a Christian Home," *Info for Families* (blog), November 13, 2013, www.infoforfamilies .com/blog/2013/11/13/how-to-raise-a-pagan-kid-in-a-christian-home #.U_EbXuBETwc=.

4. Phil Vischer, interview by Megan Basham, "It's Not about the Dream," *World*, September 24, 2011, www.worldmag.com/2011/09/it _s_not_about_the_dream/page2.

5. A. W. Tozer, *I Call It Heresy!: Twelve Timely Themes from First Peter* (Camp Hill, PA: Christian Publications, 1991), 11.

6. John H. Coe, "Resisting the Temptation of Moral Formation: Moving from Moral to Spiritual Formation" (lecture, Talbot School of Theology, Biola University, La Mirada, CA, 2009). Used with permission.

CHAPTER 4: ESSENTIAL THREE: SCRIPTURE IS OUR AUTHORITY

1. Timothy Keller, *The Meaning of Marriage: Facing the Complexities of Commitment with the Wisdom of God* (New York: Dutton, 2011), 44.

2. The Timothy Keller Sermon Archive, Logos Bible Software (New York: Redeemer Presbyterian Church, 2013).

3. Kenda Creasy Dean, *Almost Christian: What the Faith of Our Teenagers Is Telling the American Church* (Oxford: Oxford University Press, 2010), 12.

4. Dietrich Bonhoeffer, *The Cost of Discipleship* (New York: Touchstone, 1995), 89.

5. Bill Dogterom (sermon, ROCKHARBOR Church, Costa Mesa, CA, 2013). Used with permission.

CHAPTER 5: ESSENTIAL FOUR: THE HOLY SPIRIT TEACHES

1. Francis Chan, *Forgotten God: Reversing Our Tragic Neglect of the Holy Spirit* (Colorado Springs: David C Cook, 2009), 50.

2. Chan, *Forgotten God*, 15–18, 32.

3. John H. Coe, "Resisting the Temptation of Moral Formation: Moving from Moral to Spiritual Formation" (lecture, Talbot School of Theology, Biola University, La Mirada, CA, 2009). Used with permission.

CHAPTER 6: ESSENTIAL FIVE: GOD'S GRAND REDEMPTIVE NARRATIVE

1. John H. Westerhoff III, *Will Our Children Have Faith?*, rev. ed. (Harrisburg, PA: Morehouse, 2000), 7.

2. Randy Frazee, *The Heart of the Story: God's Masterful Design to Restore His People* (Grand Rapids, MI: Zondervan, 2011), 6.

3. Max Lucado, *Great House of God: A Home for Your Heart* (Nashville: Thomas Nelson, 1997), 14.

CHAPTER 7: ESSENTIAL SIX: GOD IS CENTRAL

1. Ralph Waldo Emerson, adapted by Chaim Stern, ed., *Gates of Understanding*, vol. 1 (New York: Central Conference of American Rabbis, 1977), 216.

2. Jon Acuff's equation goes like this: 1,000 compliments + 1 insult = 1 insult. *Start: Punch Fear in the Face, Escape Average, Do Work That Matters* (Brentwood, TN: Lampo, 2013), 152.

CHAPTER 8: ESSENTIAL SEVEN: A COMMUNITY OF MINISTRY SUPPORT

1. Edward Everett Hale, quoted in *Addresses of the President of the United States and the Director of the Bureau of the Budget* (Washington, DC: United States Government Printing Office, 1922), 14.

2. C. S. Lewis, *The Great Divorce* (New York: Macmillan, 1946).

3. George Barna, quoted in "Research Shows That Spiritual Maturity Process Should Start at a Young Age," Barna Group, November 17, 2003, www.barna.org/barna-update/article/5-barna-update/130-research -shows-that-spiritual-maturity-process-should-start-at-a-young-age #.VPYMZEJzr8v.

CHAPTER 9: GETTING SET TO LEAD A NEW GENERATION

1. John Stott, "The Call of Christ to Leadership," Cru.Comm, April 2012, http://crupressgreen.com/wp-content/uploads/2012/04/stott thecallofchristtoleadership.pdf.

2. Timothy Keller, *Center Church: Doing Balanced, Gospel-Centered Ministry in Your City* (Grand Rapids, MI: Zondervan, 2012), 383.

3. Michelle Anthony, *Becoming a Spiritually Healthy Family: Avoiding the 6 Dysfunctional Parenting Styles* (Colorado Springs: David C Cook, 2015), 11.

4. Michelle Anthony, *Spiritual Parenting: An Awakening for Today's Families* (Colorado Springs: David C Cook, 2010).

5. William Bridges, *Managing Transitions: Making the Most of Change*, 3rd ed. (Boston: Da Capo, 2009), 60.

6. John P. Kotter, *Leading Change* (Cambridge, MA: Harvard Business School Press, 1996), 68.

7. Seth Godin, *Tribes: We Need You to Lead Us* (New York: Portfolio, 2008), 136.

Be Empowered in Your Role as a Parent

Spiritual Parenting

creates spiritual environments that God can use to work in the lives of your children. It's a biblical, innovative, and fresh approach to parenting. Be inspired as the primary nurturer of your child's faith as you learn to practically create space for God-encounters in everyday life.

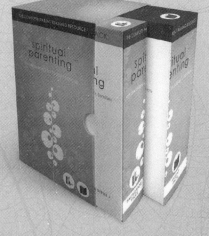

Awaken the Families in Your Church!

Spiritual Parenting is a six-part program that empowers parents to be the primary nurturers of their children's faith. Families will be transformed as they learn how to create space for God-encounters in everyday life.

Perfect for parenting classes, mom groups, mid-week, retreats, and more!

Envision
a **NEW GENERATION**
who know **GOD'S WORD,** *desire*
to **OBEY HIM,** *and respond to* **GOD**
through the **POWER** *of the* **HOLY SPIRIT**

You are impassioned for a new generation and believe that God wants to captivate the hearts of today's children and families. *Tru Curriculum offers the ministry resources that will allow you to have confidence that you are developing lifetime faith in a new generation.*

 **NEW AGE LEVEL!**
TRUIDENTITY FOR MIDDLE SCHOOLERS

Do you want to **transform the lives of teens,** empower parents, and connect with a community of like-minded ministry leaders? TruIdentity equips leaders and families with how to do ministry, not just what to teach.

transforming lives together